TOTO
&
COCO

TOTO

KOOPMAN

&

COCO

CHANEL

Spies, seduction
and the fight
for survival

ALAN FRAME

Published by

Kelvin House

CONTENTS

FOREWORD 1

WITHOUT WHOM 3

ACKNOWLEDGMENTS 5

INTRODUCTION 7

PART ONE: IT WAS THE BEST OF TIMES

Chapter 1 – Privilege, Prudery and Prejudice 11

Chapter 2 – Paris, City of Light 19

Chapter 3 – The Scent of Anti-Semitism 35

Chapter 4 – The Mad, Bad, Dangerous Tallulah 46

Chapter 5 – The Brilliant, Brutal Beaver 56

Chapter 6 – A Very Odd Couple 72

Chapter 7 – The Viscount, and Other Lovers 83

Chapter 8 – Keeping it in the Family 87

Chapter 9 – The Apprentice Spy 109

Chapter 10 – The Drums of War 118

PART TWO: IT WAS THE WORST OF TIMES

Chapter 11 – The Ritz or the Mountain Lair 142

Chapter 12 – Two Lives, Two Paths 156

Chapter 13 – Agent Westminster 162

Chapter 14 – For the Want of Aircraft 166

Chapter 15 – Hidden in Plain Sight 179

Chapter 16 – This Hell on Earth 191

Chapter 17 – Meanwhile at the Ritz 200

Chapter 18 – Not Fit for the Master Race 204

Chapter 19 – Contacts in High Places 209

Chapter 20 – One Last Card to Play 215

Chapter 21 – The Horizontal Gambler 223

Chapter 22 – The Final Order 226

PART THREE: IT WAS THE SPRING OF HOPE

Chapter 23 – Lies and Truth 234

Chapter 24 – Onions, Garlic and a Wig 242

Chapter 25 – The Papers, Letter Writing and Rest 246

Chapter 26 – The Cost of Exile 249

Chapter 27 – A Chance Meeting 253

Chapter 28 – Enter Francis Bacon 256

Chapter 29 – From Riches to Riches 262

Chapter 30 – Toto, Once More Amused, and Amusing 265

Chapter 31 – When Her Mighty Men Fell 269

Chapter 32 – No Fond Farewells 274

EPILOGUE 277

INDEX 278

BIBLIOGRAPHY 283

For Anna & Helen

FOREWORD

In my career in Fleet Street I was fortunate to have had a box seat at some of the most seismic events of the second half of the 20th century. I met the great, the good and the plain bloody awful: Princess Diana made eyes at me; Prince Philip was appallingly rude to me (in that respect I joined a very large club); and Mick Jagger made fun of me. But the greatest person I *never* met was Toto Koopman. In fact, until a year ago, I had never even heard of her. Then one evening I was introduced to her extraordinary story by the Aitken family, the descendants of Lord Beaverbrook, the genius behind the Express Newspapers empire.

I was lucky to have the help of Beaverbrook's granddaughter, Laura Aitken, as not only had she a treasure trove of letters and notes, but had met Toto in 1986 and all quoted content from Toto is based on the conversation they had.

After months of research, and a trawl through those papers, one other name kept cropping up: Coco Chanel. She is rightly acknowledged as a brilliant innovator who changed how women dressed and the perfume they wore. Less well known are her other activities… the polar opposite of her friend Toto's.

I quickly realised that if the players in this story had not existed, no invention of them could have done them justice. At its core, this is a story of good and evil, of allegiance and betrayal. But, like all good stories, there is more, so much more…

WITHOUT WHOM

My task of writing *Toto & Coco* was made so much easier thanks to the hard work and scrupulous research by the author Jean-Noel Liaut, whose *The Many Lives of Miss K* (Rizzoli) introduced readers to Toto for the first time in 2011. That fine book provided me with a brilliant framework of the life – indeed, the *many* lives – of this remarkable woman.

But missing from M Liaut's work were the revelations of Coco Chanel's activities as a Nazi agent, which came after the publication of *Miss K*. For me, the contrast of how these two women, once friends, chose to conduct themselves during the World War II was the real story; or as that most instinctive of newspaper men Lord Beaverbrook himself might have said: 'Now, that's the drama!'

The finest account of Chanel's role as one of Hitler's agents is Hal Vaughan's masterly *Sleeping with the Enemy* (Vintage), and I am indebted to him for bringing the shocking facts together so readably.

And my huge thanks (and admiration) go to Sarah Helm, whose extraordinarily detailed work on the horrors of Ravensbruck concentration camp – *If This is a Woman* (Hachette) – is quite simply a masterpiece of research and reporting.

ACKNOWLEDGEMENTS

Few books are truly solo efforts; rather they are born out of a mix of encouragement and cajoling from friends and family.

So, my sincere thanks go to many, particularly my editor, the brilliant Kimberley Miller, whose calm and wise presence is reflected throughout this work. She really is the 'editor's editor'.

James Willis of SpiffingCovers has been an endless source of advice; my great friend Robert Thackery was kind enough to read the first draft and offer his suggestions, all of which were gratefully followed.

I am grateful for the friendship of Will Liley, Nigel Coulter, Nigel Jackson and Brian Basham and the love of my daughters Anna and Helen.

Gratitude also goes to Toby Gough, Jonathan Kenworthy for the story of the Cherkley Radio Shack, to Mala Tribich who knew only too well the horrors of Ravensbruck, and to the late Jean Farnfield for her memories of Beaverbrook.

Nicole Patterson was my invaluable legal eagle, and

of course gratitude goes to Laura Aitken for sharing her 'little box of treasures': the notes and letters to and from Toto, Beaverbrook and her father Max.

If I have forgotten anyone, my sincere apologies.

Finally, I will forever be thankful to my 'Chief of Staff', Jeanette Bishop, for her unfailing help and support.

INTRODUCTION
BY JODIE KIDD

As a little girl one of my great treats was visiting my cousin Laura on the Isle of Wight, where she sailed and raced powerboats just like her father, Sir Max Aitken. It was there that I first saw the portrait of a truly beautiful woman, painted by the famed Joseph Oppenheimer. The picture fascinated me, and still does; it has a haunting quality which draws the viewer into the soul of the subject. Who is she? I used to wonder.

Toto Koopman intrigued me then as I believe she will captivate you now. The era in which she reigned supreme, the 1930s, was so stylish and glamorous, and full of the most outrageous and fun people. But there is another reason for my intense interest in this remarkable woman: six decades later, I too became a Chanel model, and was the Face of Chanel. But the connection is far deeper than that. Her life was dominated and irrevocably changed by my family: great grandfather, Lord Beaverbrook, and his son Max. If Toto had never met them, would we be reading about her now?

As for the other main player in this drama, we might think that Coco Chanel needs no introduction. But we would be wrong. And it is the way the lives of these two women, once good friends, diverged so dramatically that makes this story so utterly gripping.

PART ONE

IT WAS THE BEST OF TIMES

CHAPTER 1

PRIVILEGE, PRUDERY AND PREJUDICE

Java, full of light, of mysticism and mystery. It shaped me...'

— Toto

Flickering black and white, the figures on the screen paced, eyes wild and gestures melodramatic. It was the first film – a silent movie – seven-year-old Catherina Johanna Anna Koopman had seen. She was spellbound.

The year was 1915, and the 'cinema' was a little wooden village hall on the outskirts of Salatiga in the mountainous heartlands of Java in the Indian Ocean. The motion picture, shown as a weekly serial in nine episodes, was *The Perils of Pauline*, and the opening episode was called 'Trial by Fire'. Others, like 'Goddess of the Far West', 'Deadly Turning' and 'Tragic Plunge' followed. She could not have known it then, of course, but the films were a portent of sorts, seeming to predict the 'life less ordinary' that stretched out before the young Miss Koopman.

The heroine of the series, Pauline, was played by the spirited actress Pearl White, and the plot daring for the time: Pauline is the ward of her wealthy guardian, Mr Marvin, who leaves all of his money to her to be realised on her marriage – to his son Harry. She refuses, hell-bent instead on adventure, travelling the world and becoming a writer. The entire inheritance is entrusted to Marvin's secretary who, unbeknown to the kindly man, is a crook, determined to get the millions for himself… so determined that he plots to have the intrepid Pauline killed while on her travels.

Even sat here, in the 21st century, it is easy to see why Catherina would have been enthralled by such a plot. But the life of the young viewer, sat wide-eyed and transfixed in the front row, was to be more exciting still, and featured not a celluloid heroine but a real-life one.

Catharina was a child of colonial privilege, born on 28th October 1908 in Salatiga, where her father was a cavalry colonel in the Dutch East Indies army. The tropical island had been ruled by the Dutch since 1814, and as a child of the ruling class she was surrounded by turbaned Javanese servants, all immaculately dressed and impeccably mannered. And then there was Djim, her adored Indonesian nanny, in starched jacket and enormous earrings. But most startling about Djim was her teeth, sharpened with a file and stained jet-black from the betel nuts she constantly chewed.

When her parents, Jan George and Catharina, went to have her birth registered, the chosen name for their daughter – Toto, after her father's favourite horse – was rejected. So Catharina she became instead, after her mother, but it was rarely used, and never by the family. Her older sibling Henry was also known by another name – Ody – and despite the six-year age gap, big brother and little sister were very close. Ody was Toto's protector and her champion, always taking her side when she got into scrapes, which she did often. A tree climber and lover of snakes – some of which, like the blue temple viper, were highly venomous – Catherina appeared to know no fear. This led to the first real confrontation with her father, who sat her down and read her the riot act, warning her that she would be confined to the house if she disobeyed his order to not go near any snakes, for any reason whatsoever. The disgruntled Toto obeyed, but it was the first challenge of her love of independence and daring – traits, for good or bad, which never left her.

Java is one of the most beautiful places on earth, blessed with a perfect temperate climate, fertile tropical rainforests, high mountain peaks, fields of barley, and birds of every colour. The Koopman house was surrounded by lush lawns, lakes and nearby rice paddies, coffee and tea plantations; and, in the distance, volcanic mountains and the largest Buddhist temple in the world, Borobudur, built over 75 years in the ninth century and made even more mystical by being buried by volcanic ash until its rediscovery by the British adventurer Sir Stamford Raffles 600 years later.

This extraordinary monument to Buddhist beliefs appears from afar to be a small city built on a hill., The temple's relief panels, more than 2,600 of them, depict, among many other things, the horrors of hell and the ecstasies of heaven – concepts Toto would later have much cause to reflect on. By the time Toto was old enough to visit Borobudur for the first time, restoration by the Dutch had started, exposing almost 600 statues of the Buddha carved from stone. Even for a childish Toto, it was an awesome sight, and a feeling now shared by the millions who have visited the temple since. Today it is a world heritage site and a place of worship once more.

The island has a spiritual quality too, almost ethereal, as a result of the centuries of Buddhism and Hinduism. Toto was fascinated by the sounds and smells in which Java was steeped; the muffle of the temple bell and the scent of incense were hypnotic and left her with a lasting interest in the mystical. In particular, she was intrigued by the legend of Ratu Kidul, the mythical queen of the southern sea of Java, variously thought of as a ghostly goddess, half woman and half mermaid, and very beautiful. She was said to take the soul of whoever she chose and, in the case of fishermen, did so with tragic regularity.

When Toto was old enough she and her mother, always dressed in white, would cycle to the lake to swim. The family also rode horses together most days, Mrs Koopman side-saddle. Toto had a Java pony, a small but tough little thing bred for working in the fields, and very different to the prize steeds in Col Koopman's stables. But she had fallen too many times, eventually breaking a hip, and preferred her bicycle. Alas, her father's dream of her as an Olympic showjumper was not to be. Would she make him proud in a different way?

If it seemed the idyllic life, it was. Almost. But there was one issue with the idyll: Mrs Koopman was not pure Dutch as her husband was. She was born Catharina Westrik in 1880 to Dutch and Indonesian parents. She also had Chinese ancestry, and the Chinese were very much considered – and indeed still are – the 'shop-keeping class' of Indonesia, and definitely lacking the pedigree of the smart colonials. There was worse: a grandmother was said, fancifully perhaps, to have been part of the Sultan of Solo's harem. Sultans (or kings) once ruled the island[1], and were regarded as almost divine figures, and had many wives. For the prudish, pious Protestant Dutch at the time, this mixed marriage was bordering on sinful, and children born of it were known as 'Green Dutch' after the colour of their skin – except their skin wasn't remotely green, it was a beautiful shade of brown. As a consequence, the so-called Green Dutch were subject to blatant racism and prejudice.

The children were schooled at home by a governess employed by the regiment until they were 12 and enrolled in their respective boarding schools in Holland. Toto was a bright child and by the age of eight could

[1] The current Sultan of Solo spends his days smoking menthol cigarettes and sipping espresso in a hotel coffee shop in Java…

converse in French and English, in addition to Dutch, the family's first language. She was also able to speak a little Indonesian with the family servants, and had a natural ability to absorb the sounds and rhythms of a new language. By the time she enrolled at Bloemendaal in Holland, she spoke excellent French and English, and was learning German. She'd also started to learn Italian, a language she loved because of the passion and romance she associated it with.

Ody and Toto's parents protected their children well, and it was only upon arrival at boarding school that they were exposed to any form of prejudice when some of their fellow pupils began to taunt them, as children are prone to do when they know no better. They were quickly silenced, and Toto would in fact play up her exotic heritage, with emphasis *on* the sultan's harem! (Years later, Toto would reflect that being subjected to the ignorance of others at such a young age helped toughen her character.)

Toto's father was responsible for buying horses for the cavalry regiment, and his main source was Australia, which meant he was away for much of the time. But he always returned bearing gifts. One was particularly exotic, at least for Java: a kangaroo. Toto was very proud indeed, and the envy of children from other cavalry families. And when the King of Siam visited Java, Col Koopman acted as his aide-de-camp. His reward was a baby elephant, which Toto named Jambo – another exotic member of her growing menagerie. In one respect, Buddhism had left its mark on the young Toto: she adored all animals (including snakes) and believed them to be part of the human family and not to be killed, though she was not a vegetarian.

> *'I was so happy as a little girl. I suppose I was a bit spoiled, and the only unhappiness I remember was having to say goodbye to Jambo, my elephant, when he grew too big and had to go to a zoo in Jakarta. And when Ody was sent off to school when he was 12 and I was only six. I really missed him. We were all worried about him, as he reached Holland just as the Great War began. But he wrote to us regularly, and he went through it unscathed, emerging as the school's tennis champion. Otherwise, my childhood on Java was my little piece of paradise, and I had everything. My freedom, pets, friends and wonderful parents. And Java, full of light, of mysticism and mystery. It shaped me...'*
>
> – Toto in 1986, aged 78, speaking about her childhood to Laura Aitken, granddaughter of Lord Beaverbrook and daughter of Sir Max Aitken, whose lives, as we shall see, became inextricably intertwined with her own.

The time had come for her to leave this Eden behind, however, and follow her brother to Holland, where her new life at Bloemendaal, a very traditional all-girls boarding school, began. At 12, Toto was now a striking young woman, with several advantages over the other new girls in that she was already supremely confident, undeniably beautiful, with a hint of the exotic, and very clever. If some thought her inferior because she was bi-racial, they were simply dispatched – and they most certainly didn't return for more. Her best friend and kindred spirit was Kajsa Wust, with whom she enjoyed an early and tentative lesbian foray. Both girls enjoyed school and the high academic standards, but not Holland in the 1920s. It too was ruled by strict, straight-laced Protestants, and far too puritanical for their liking.

When Toto was 17 she left for London to do what most girls of her class did back then: learn to be a lady. Her parents enrolled her at Miss Crozier's Finishing School in Knightsbridge, the sort of establishment which was usually found in Switzerland. There, the daughters of privilege were taught deportment, polite conversation and manners, flower arranging and basic cooking skills – or at least how to plan a menu with one's cook. Toto considered it all rather silly and giggled a lot…and couldn't wait to move on.

When she emerged she was refined, and knew how to sashay through the admiring glances of both men and women; but she was also well educated, a considerable linguist, and hungry for the world.

The young lady from one of the world's most volcanic countries was about to embark on a life which would be no less volcanic, and there was only one place on earth made for her, and she made for it: Paris.

CHAPTER 2

PARIS, CITY OF LIGHT

'I grew up very quickly…'

– Toto

Paris. June 1928. Cold and wet, and as un-Parisian and miserable a day as one could imagine. But Toto wasn't put off. She had been to the city several times before; once with her father and, at other times, with school friends from Holland. On one trip, they feasted on the naked physique of some lesser-known Athenian warrior captured in marble in a museum…and Toto recalled her intense irritation at the childish giggling of her classmates. Even aged 13, Toto was something of a sophisticate, it seems. And now, weather aside, she was about to call Paris home at a time when it was a city revelling in *les années folles* – the crazy years.

A decade earlier, at the end of the Great War, the elegant French capital had been a shadow of its former glorious self; but by the late 1920s the French economy was booming, the slums of the old century had been replaced in almost every suburb, and employment was high. It was a city riding proud on the hosting of the Paris Olympics – at which Germany was banned – and Charles Lindbergh making history when he landed at Le Bourget after his solo flight from New York. Everyone, it seemed, was dropping in on the City of Light. The place was also the centre of the artistic universe: the writers Yeats, Hemingway and Ezra Pound were there; George Orwell was washing up in kitchens as research for *Down and Out in Paris and London*. And Painters Picasso and Dali, and composers Erik Sati, Ravel and Stravinsky, were all extravagant components of this mad, vibrant scene.[2]

Still only 19, and without her parents' full approval (but with their financial support), Toto was determined to escape her smothering, privileged upbringing and make a life of her own. She was as elegant as any woman gracing the city, with a full mouth, wide green eyes, small breasts and a long, slim body. Poised, ambitious and with the self-confidence of a woman far older, she was more than ready to immerse herself in the extravagance and culture of the French capital. There were also upwards of 80 couture houses at work in the city, and Toto was determined to become a model and, no less so, a fixture in the famed Parisian café society and its intoxicating mix of the bohemian and international. The late 1920s

---

[2] There was also one man who was not part of that set: Ho Chi Minh, future leader of Vietnam, was honing his revolutionary skills while working as a pastry chef (and, by all accounts, a very good one).

was the perfect time for a beautiful and vivacious young woman to be in Paris.

She found a small apartment on the wide, tree-lined Boulevard Berthier in the 17th arrondissement – not the most fashionable address, but smart enough.[3] The American portraitist John Singer Sargent had lived nearby, and the actor Preston Sturges would move in later. Many Russians had fled to the city in the wake of the Revolution (several of the old Tsarist aristocrats were eking out a living driving cabs) along with thousands of Armenians, Czechs and Slovacs. It was a heady cultural brew, and after the horrors of a world war and a bloody revolution it made for a society keen to live only for the day because, well, tomorrow, who knew…

Politically, Paris reflected the extremes of much of the rest of Europe: Fascism and Communism on the rise in Germany, Spain and Italy, and the Communists in full control of Russia, by then the Soviet Union. Violent protestors from the Right and Left had been on the march, but the residual agitation was of no consequence to a woman determined to write the rules of her own life and seek those whose paths were on the same trajectory as her own…that of modelling.

Many of the couture brands that still lead the world today were born in the city during this period, where names like Dior, Rochas, Schiaparelli and Mainbocher all competed to dress the beautiful, the rich and the

---

[3] The building now houses a dry cleaning and ironing shop (on the ground floor), and sadly arrived too late for Toto's patronage.

famous. And, of course, Chanel… But what made Paris so special? Practically speaking, there was an abundance of highly skilled seamstresses; but the real driver was the city's love of the arts and the *laissez faire* approach to life which, by night, was inventive and risqué.

Wasting not a moment, Toto got herself in front of a camera to compile a portfolio of pictures she hoped would be her entrée into the modelling world. Just a short time after, she met Gabrielle Chanel, known to all as Coco and acknowledged as the high priestess of fashion and by then fabulously wealthy through her designs and her Chanel No 5 perfume. Chanel immediately hired Toto as her house model. But more than that: it was a meeting which would have huge and lasting consequences for both women.

Coco and Toto were almost social equals, with Coco already the essence of French chic; but their backgrounds, and personalities, could not have been more different. Now aged 47, more than twice Toto's age, Chanel was the illegitimate daughter of peasant parents.[4] By the age of 12 she was motherless, and by 20 a seamstress, and seemingly destined for a life of drudgery had it not been for her burning will to succeed at any cost…particularly when that cost was borne by others, as we will go on to reveal.

---

[4] Chanel would often romanticise her past, creating a far more glamorous version that included her father sailing to America to seek his fortune after her mother's death. She also told people she was born a decade later than she was.

What Toto lacked in cash and cachet she made up for with her beguiling presence, her beauty, her spirit of adventure and independence, and her intelligence (she was now fluent in five languages), traits which enchanted both men and women of all ages. By contrast, Chanel was severe-looking and without warmth. But she was in possession of a ruthless ambition which, combined with a supreme talent for design, made her the beating heart of Parisian haute couture; indeed, her ability to understand the *je ne sais quoi* of future trends was extraordinary. Her position and wealth[5] made her a must-have guest at all the best parties.

Chanel was fascinated by Toto. Her new, young friend was everything she wanted to be, but wasn't – beautiful, slightly exotic, confident and poised – and she made sure Toto received an invitation to every party she went to. Chanel was bisexual, and as far as Toto was concerned, why abandon her tentative dormitory exploration of lesbianism just because men were on the scene?

But the attraction was distinctly one way. Toto was not drawn to Chanel, and thought her cold and demanding. Nothing must get in the way of the 'Great Chanel' and after six months of working as her house model Toto left, telling friends that she did not like the

---

[5] But she was not as rich as her latest lover, the Duke of Westminster, Hugh Grosvenor, unofficial leader of the British Adolf Hitler admiration society. By his outrageous standards, she was still a pauper.

way Coco constantly touched her during fittings. As she related to Laura Aitken: *'I left partly for that reason, but also because it was time to move on. Though we seemed to be friends, I really didn't much like Coco, she could be very cold. In fact, she was a bully. She wasn't fun and that's what I was looking for at that age.'*

But Toto's time at Chanel's headquarters in Rue Cambon served her well and she was immediately in demand, working for Marcel Rochas and for the American couturier Main Rousseau Bocher, whose brand was and still is known as Mainbocher.[6] He soon became her favourite designer, and he told Vogue that he aimed to make clothes that were 'a friend to women; the kind of friend you can see again and again and not get sick of.'

Another favourite of Toto was Rochas, whose motto was 'Youth, Simplicity, Personality'. He was the inventor of the trouser suit, and became famous for the wide shoulders which soon became *de rigeur*; and, like his rival Chanel, he branched out into the perfume market.

Toto's work for Mainbocher made her the go-to model, and three years after arriving in Paris she was the favourite subject of one of the greatest photographers of the day: George Hoyningen-Huene of French Vogue. Hoyningen-Huene, the only son of a Baltic baron and chief equerry to Tsar Alexander, was one of the many

---

[6] Mainbocher was a WW1 veteran who, posing as a music student, exposed and broke up a network of drug traffickers who were supplying narcotics to American airmen.

Russian emigres in the city.[7] He worked in huge studios with Ionic columns, in contrast with the images of factory chimneys and railway tunnels.

It was against this extraordinary backdrop that Toto shone, modelling creations from Madame Gres, Madame Vionnet and Chanel, and looking like 'a vision in a dream', according to one admiring critic. She wore minimalist dresses that accentuated her curves, and powdered her body so the fabric would not cling. Recounting those days, Toto said memorably: *'I dressed not for men, but to astound women…'*

Toto had become the toast of the City of Style, and the first bi-racial model to achieve what would now be considered celebrity status. She moved out of her modest apartment in Boulevard Berthier, and elected to live in whichever fashionable hotel caught her fancy: sometimes the Ritz, where Coco Chanel had taken up residence; at other times the chic San Regis on Rue Jean Goujon. The most iconic photograph of her by Hoyningen-Huene, and one of the most memorable of the decade, shows her from behind, focusing on her delicate neck and hips, her face hidden. She also posed for Horst, later Hoyningen-Huene's male lover, and Cecil Beaton, who became the favourite photographer of the British royal family and the stars of Hollywood. Her acquired wealth (she had to be wealthy to afford the finest hotels in Paris), coupled with her sexual

---

[7] The family fled the Bolsheviks, first to London and later to Paris.

freedom and style, had become her passport to Paris 'high society'.

Despite no longer working for her, Toto spent many evenings in Coco's company, simply because they were part of 'the set': film director Alexander Korda, Tallulah Bankhead, Jean Cocteau, Picasso, Salvador Dali, Man Ray, and the surrealist visual artist and his lover Lee Miller. Miller was a beautiful New Yorker, a year older than Toto and, like her, a great favourite of Vogue.[8] Man Ray and Miller were an outrageous couple, often seen strolling through the city streets linked to each other by a gold chain around their waists; more disturbingly, Miller would carry around a silver tray on which she had placed a knife, fork, salt and pepper shakers…and a severed woman's breast, which she had somehow obtained from a medical school. The set was rarely without one or more of the Mdivani siblings too, who were an outrageous concoction of fakery (they claimed to be Russian royalty), burning ambition and sex, and the forebears of the Kardashian family. The term 'famous for being famous' might well have been invented for the likes of the Mdivanis! Toto could not resist them, and they could not resist her.

Just as Toto and Coco were the must-haves on every guest list, so too were Alexis, David and Serge Mdivani, and their sisters Nina and Roussy. Their father,

---

[8] In many ways their lives ran in parallel in that they were uninhibited, were fixtures at every party, and would later play their parts in the forthcoming war.

General Zakhari Mdivani, had been aide-de-camp to Tsar Nicholas, and in 1921 fled Russia with his family as the newly created Soviet army invaded Georgia, their homeland. (They apparently left behind a small house in Tblisi, and a flock of sheep. Hardly the trappings of great nobility…) They were first noticed in Paris in 1923, by which time Mdivani senior had sold the family jewels to realise enough money to survive. The children had three great assets: they were all very good looking, they were shameless, and they were imaginative enough to play out the story of the Russian royalty they claimed to be. Not only did these imposters need money, they craved it. Yet Paris society welcomed the three Mdivani princes and the equally bogus little princesses. In the days before social media and the internet, who was to know for sure that the titles were pure fiction? As their father was later to say: 'I must be the only father to inherit a title from my sons…'

'Prince' Alexis had an affair with Toto, but not before accumulating a fortune by marrying, first, Louise Astor Van Alen, great niece of John Jacob Astor. For Mdivani, his marriage to Louise was just long enough to get his hands on the Astor money, spending it on the most lavish parties – at which his wife was rarely seen – and playing polo with the Prince of Wales and Prince Louis of Battenberg, the future Lord Mountbatten… two real princes. Aside from this exhausting, fully funded life of leisure, Alexis had been in receipt of some rather astonishing wedding presents from his wife: a stable of prized polo ponies, 30 suits to cater for every season and occasion, diamond and pearl shirt studs, and a new Rolls-Royce. His father-in-law, though doubtful of his daughter's choice, had also given him a speedboat. Soon after the wedding they decamped to Biarritz – or rather Alexis did, as Louise was never seen there.

The marriage lasted little more than a year, during which time Alexis was already wooing his next victim: Louise's closest friend, 20-year-old Barbara Hutton of the Woolworth empire, regarded as the richest heiress in the US. (He was certainly not interested in doing anything as grubby as work.)

He knew that Hutton was about to turn 21, the age at which she would inherit her grandfather's bequest – the equivalent today of £700 million. It was enough to keep Alexis Mdivani firmly focused. In 1933, Louise caught Alexis in bed with Hutton. But it was Alexis' sister Roussy who had ensured that Louise would catch them. The whole thing had been choreographed by Miss Mdivani so that her brother would wind up divorced – the marriage had lasted little more than a year – allowing him to immediately move on to Hutton and the next pot of gold. The marriage cost Louise – or, more accurately, her father – £8 million, which was mere chicken feed compared with his next target.

Barbara Hutton confirmed to the Syracuse Journal newspaper in New York State that she would be 'victim number two' (though that's not the phrase she used) telling them: 'I like the life Alexis lives. All the American men I know are businessmen, and once they marry a girl they wrap themselves in business again. Alexis is amusing, smart and interesting. It won't be like marrying a foreigner at all, since he is a real cosmopolitan. It is mean of people to say that Alexis is following my millions around the world.' Mean maybe, but entirely accurate definitely.

The couple married in the Russian cathedral in Paris in June that year, and embarked on a honeymoon fit for a 'prince' and his new princess. The New York Times reported: 'No bride anywhere at any time could have been lovelier than this dainty blonde. She was more than radiant, she was positively angelic.' And quoting the new 'Princess' Barbara Mdivani: 'Alexis is smart, cute, amusing, interesting, and hangs around all the time.' To which some wag observed: 'Sounds like a good Irish setter.'

On their first night on the train to Lake Como, Mdivani failed to live up to Barbara's New York Times appraisal of her new prince and told his bride that she was too fat, whereupon she embarked upon a crash diet, consuming, it was reported, nothing more than three cups of black coffee a day. She lost 46 pounds in weight, but it nearly killed her. From Como they went to Venice and took the royal suite (what else?) at the Excelsior on the Lido; then was time for another boat, this time a powerful American Chris-Craft, a wedding present from his new father-in-law Franklyn Hutton, complete with a crew of three. They threw the most extravagant parties, where guests included no less than *les mademoiselles* Coco Chanel and Toto Koopman.

Toto…

Suddenly the groom was on the prowl again and, on his return to Paris, the pair become lovers.

Toto said she was drawn to Alexis and his siblings because of their lifestyle, which she considered '*an expression of intellectual and erotic independence. Pleasure without guilt.*' She might have added: *And other people's money*. She liked their titles, and decided she needed one herself, but not by marrying – no, she made it clear that she wanted neither a husband nor children – but by invention. So she became 'Baroness van Halmaell'. Her nephew Robbert (the Dutch spelling) Koopman said: 'Toto researched the family tree and discovered that an ancestor, Jan George Koopman (1770-1830), married Maria van Halmaell, who was from wealthy Belgian nobility.' It was another case of Toto writing the rules for her life: she did what she liked; she lived how she liked; she went to bed with whom she liked. In other words, she lived like most of the men she knew. She appears not to have been one for the sisterhood however, as, if she wanted to, she would also sleep with the husbands, or indeed the wives, of friends.

She and Alexis thought nothing of being seen in public, and went out every night, fuelled on champagne – and probably the drug of choice, cocaine – or spent time on Mdivani's latest toy, the yacht *Ali-Baba* (named after the blessed union of Alexis and Barbara, now fractured). They also holidayed in Spain, staying with Alexis' sister

Roussy and her husband, the Catalan artist Josep Maria Sert, the richest painter of his day, arriving there on the *Ali-Baba*.

In the space of less than two years, and with Toto a very visible part of his life, Alexis and the gullible Hutton had behaved like the travelling royalty they were not, with 'state visits' (their words) to China and India, as well as Europe and the United States. In that time they had spent much of her enormous inheritance, and Alexis' alcohol consumption had increased alarmingly. After one evening in the Embassy, London's most fashionable nightclub of the time and patronised by the Prince of Wales and countless louche aristocrats, Alexis was arrested for 'being disorderly' and spent the night cooling off in a police cell. The newspapers were full of the story, and within days Barbara suffered a breakdown and was admitted to a London nursing home. Her parents headed over to be with her…whilst Alexis went to play polo at Roehampton, with Toto arriving from Paris to watch the match.

Inevitably, Alexis' second and very lucrative marriage ended in divorce in March 1935. He still had Toto, however, and there was another heiress on his arm, one who would live the rest of her life regretting ever setting eyes on the man: Maud Thyssen. Maud was 23 years old and married to the German industrialist Baron Thyssen, 40 years her senior. She and Alexis had been staying in Spain with the Serts, just as he and Toto had previously. Maud was due to catch a flight, and Mdivani decided to drive her to the airport. Speeding through Albons in Catalonia in his silver-grey open-topped Rolls-Royce Phantom, with the British registration ALF 222, he lost control of the car at high speed.

The International News Service reported: 'According to an eyewitness, Mdivani was almost decapitated in the crash when his car turned over. The eyewitness to the tragedy, Jose de Palou, said: "I was driving along the Figueroa-Palamos Highway when an open Rolls-Royce thundered past me, driven by a man, apparently naked from the waist up. I estimated the speed of the car at about 80 miles an hour. Suddenly the automobile turned over completely, five times, falling upside down on the road. I found Alexis with his head pinned to the ground by the windscreen, which was broken and which had almost severed his head. His companion had been thrown out of the car, flying through the air some 20 yards, and had landed in a field. Alexis was wearing blue shorts and canvas shoes."'

Maud Thyssen suffered a crushed skull and foot and lost the sight of an eye – lifelong injuries. For the bogus Prince Alexis Mdivani, it was the final journey. Left behind in the mangled Rolls was a crocodile skin case, which went everywhere with him, containing a vast collection of jewels he had acquired from his women. Left behind in the wreckage of his life were his siblings, two former wives, Toto, and dozens of other lovers. He was 30 years old. As Barbara Hutton said: 'I thought something like this might happen.'

Toto had enjoyed her time with Alexis but, as seemed to be the norm for their set, it certainly was not an exclusive relationship for either of them. She had a female lover – Tallulah Bankhead, the outrageous Hollywood star whose antics would put to shame even the worst excesses of today's headline makers – and a man who would change her life forever, Lord Beaverbrook, champion of Winston Churchill (and, very much, of himself).

As for 'Princess' Barbara, she too had gained a taste for titles and later that year would become, on marriage number two, Countess Barbara Kurt von Haugwitz-Reventlow; in 1942, plain Mrs Cary Grant; in 1947, Princess Igor Troubetzkoy; in 1953, Mrs Porfirio Rubirosa; in 1955, Baroness Gottfried von Cramn; and in 1964, Princess Pierre Raymond Doan Vinh na Champassak. Seven marriages, five grand titles, and an awful lot of family money she would never see again.

And the Mdivanis? Serge married the actress Polo Negri, star of silent film, then Hollywood actress Mary McCormack, and finally his former sister-in-law Louise Astor Van Alen (yes, really). Serge was killed in a polo accident in 1936, just months after his brother's death.

David wed the actress Mae Murray (he was her fourth husband), and reduced her from millions to penury. After their divorce, he married oil heiress Virginia Sinclair. That marriage confounded the cynics: they were still together when he died in 1984.

Roussy had just the one marriage, to Josep Maria Sert, but she died in 1938, addicted to opium and frail and broken by the tragedies, however self-inflicted, that befell her brothers.

Apart from her brother David, Nina was alone in apparently finding genuine happiness. She married Denis Conan Doyle, son of the Sherlock Holmes creator, and they stayed together until his death in 1955.

> *'I loved it. I grew up very quickly there and made many friends, some for the rest of my life.'*
>
> – Toto on Paris

CHAPTER 3

THE SCENT OF ANTI-SEMITISM

*'[…] she was too concerned with her own wealth to
worry about what was right or wrong.'*

— Toto on Coco Chanel

Far from the stable of fine pedigree horses owned by
Toto's father, Colonel Jan George Koopman, the only
horse in Gabrielle Chasnel's life — as she was originally
registered due to a slip of the quill — was the shabby old
thing that pulled her father's cart as he peddled cheap
work clothes on the streets of Saumur in France's Pays
de la Loire.

Coco's parents — Albert Chanel and Jeanne Devole
— finally married in 1884, the year after she was born;
and when her mother died, aged just 33 in 1895,
Gabrielle was the second of six children, four girls and
two boys. On Jeanne's death, the girls were put into
the Aubazine convent orphanage in Correze, Central
France. 'From that moment,' she was heard to say, 'I
knew that I was dead.' It was a miserable existence of

hard work, abysmal food and Catholic indoctrination, which included the relentless preaching of hatred for Jews who, the Sacred Heart of Mary nuns told her, were 'the source of everything wrong with the world'. After all, wasn't it they who killed our Lord? The views were not exclusive to the order; they were also shared widely throughout the country, and many blamed Judaism for the dawn of Communism.

When Gabrielle and her sisters were moved to a Catholic pension in Moulins, she was when she was put to work sewing, for a pittance and, now aged 20, began singing at a café patronised by cavalry officers for extra money.

Though far from beautiful, and lacking any timbre to her voice, Coco had something of an aura, with dark, smouldering eyes and an almost boyish figure…and attracted the attentions of one officer in particular, a rich textile heir named Etienne Balsan. She soon became his mistress, and then chatelaine of his chateau and racing stable at Compegne[9], 40 miles from Paris, where she learned to ride and later to hunt. After three years with Balsan, mastering the manners and sexual mores of the upper classes, Coco left her 'tutor' when she fell in love with his close friend, the polo-playing English aristocrat, Arthur 'Boy' Capel.

The jury is out on how or why Coco became Coco. Some say she chose the name because it is a shortened

---

[9] Once the demesne of successive French kings.

version of the French for 'kept woman', *cocotte*; others that it was from one of the songs she used to sing. Coco was heard to say that her father called her Coco, but this may have been one of her more romantic stories about her past.

It was attending polo matches with Capel that inspired the iconic Chanel blazer, for Coco had no desire to flounce around in elaborate dresses, and instead wore trousers and a boy's jacket draped around her shoulders. Impressed by her designs, Capel financed her first steps into fashion when she started designing hats, and later dresses and suits. He also paid for boutiques in Paris, Deauville and Biarritz, which would establish her reputation and where her 'Little Black Dress' made its debut. It was Capel who made House of Chanel; and it was House of Chanel that made Coco a very rich woman.

When Capel died in a car crash in 1919 she was inconsolable, and thus began a lifelong dependence on morphine. She also pursued more frequent relationships with women, though not at the neglect of affairs with men, providing they were of the rich variety. It also helped if they shared her views on the Jews.

Enter Dmitri Pavlovich, a Russian…but not any old Russian. Dmitri was a grand duke and a bisexual who had been involved in the murder of Rasputin. He'd fled to France with an impressive collection of jewels, including pearls, which would soon become Coco's trademark. But his greatest achievement, as far as his new mistress was concerned, was introducing her to his friend, a fellow Russian émigré, Ernest Beaux, who had been the Tsar's official *parfumier*. Beaux set about creating a range of fragrances for Chanel, blending synthetic and natural compounds and then labelling them by number. Initially, Coco chose number 22; but then changed her mind. 'I'll have the fifth one instead,' she said. Need we say more… Consisting of 80 ingredients in a recipe that is largely unchanged to this day, the bottle was – still is – the shape of her beloved 'Boy' Capel's hipflask.

Coco was growing richer by the day. And more anti-Semitic, thanks to the production deal she struck with the Jewish Wertheimers in 1924. She was at the Longchamp races when she met Pierre Wertheimer who, along with his brother Paul, owned Bourjois perfumes and a factory with manufacturing capacity. That afternoon a deal was struck for Bourjois to make and distribute Chanel No 5 and other scents. But it was a terrible deal, at least for Coco. It seemed on this occasion her business savvy had failed her, as she now owned just 10 per cent of the 'joint' company. But she did not put it down to her own absurd stupidity on this occasion – she'd even used Wertheimer's lawyer to draw up the agreement! – but on the fact that he was Jewish…and thus a further catalyst for her appalling views.

Coco hired Vera Bate, distantly related to the British royal family, to promote No 5 among the upper classes of the UK. And there was nobody more upper class than Vera's cousin, the Duke of Westminster.

Hugh Richard Arthur Grosvenor, second Duke of Westminster, owned vast swathes of England,

Scotland, Northern Ireland and London's most desirable areas: Mayfair, Chelsea, Westminster, Belgravia and Knightsbridge. He had 17 Rolls-Royces, two ocean-going boats (a schooner and a converted Royal Navy vessel), and a private train to bring him from the 54-bedroomed Eaton Hall, his Cheshire mansion, to Grosvenor House, his vast home in London. From birth he was known to family and friends as 'Bendor', named after his grandfather's favourite racehorse. He was wildly homophobic, and anti-Semitic…to the extent of blatant cheer-leading for Hitler. Chanel became his mistress for five years, overlapping his first and second marriages, and was wooed by daily love letters and baskets of flowers and fruit from the 11,000-acre Cheshire estate, transported to Paris by a liveried footman.

Reflective of the pedigree of her social circle, Vera Bate was also a friend of Winston Churchill, and Coco was soon being pursued not just by Grosvenor but by the Prince of Wales (later Duke of Windsor) – whose dalliances with Hitler were very well publicised – and Lord Rothermere, owner of The Daily Mail and another upper-class English Nazi apologist. They were not alone: the upper classes feared the spread of Communism throughout Europe like they feared plague and Hitler seemed, for a while at least, to be the antidote.

Winston Churchill, Hitler's absolute nemesis, was much taken by Coco when she briefly moved in as chatelaine of Eaton Hall, and the pair rode, hunted and shot together. Winston wrote to his wife Clementine:

'The famous Chanel turned up and I took great fancy to her – a most capable woman – much the stronger personality Bendor has been up against.'

Later, from Grosvenor's fishing lodge in Scotland, he told Clemmie: *'Chanel is here in place of Violet*[10] *[…] she fishes from morn to night and has killed 50 salmon (sometimes weighing 24 pounds.) She is very agreeable – really a great and strong being, fit to rule a man and an empire.'*

Coco had Churchill somewhat won over…which she would attempt to use to her favour come the end of the war.

The affair with Westminster ended in 1929, though the couple continued to see each other throughout the next decade. Coco then proved, with little doubt, that her taste for money was far stronger than her hatred of Jews.

In the summer of 1930, her grand duke introduced her to Samuel Goldwyn, the greatest Hollywood producer of the day…and born a Hassidic Jew in Warsaw. It may have been the height of the Great Depression, but that did not stop the first of the great movie moguls from luring Chanel – with almost £15 million in today's values – to spend time in Hollywood designing for his stars, foremost of whom was the gloriously glamorous actress Gloria Swanson. Goldwyn also made sure their collaboration had maximum impact by hiring the finest photographers to capture the dazzling creations: Beaton, Horst and Hoyningen-Huene, who all photographed

---

[10] Bendor's second wife.

Toto. Coco also visited New York, and Fifth Avenue in particular. But America was not to her liking, and neither were Americans; it was and they were too brash by far, though the huge increase in her bank balance was most acceptable...but it was just as well she didn't have to count all the notes; poor ill-educated Coco still had to use her fingers for adding up.

Much more to her taste was a charming German baron, Hans Gunther von Dincklage, known as 'Spatz', who posed as a tennis-loving playboy living a life of quiet luxury at Sanary-sur-Mer on the Riviera. He was indeed a playboy, in the business of cultivating a wide circle of French and British friends. But he divided his time on the Riviera with an apartment in Paris, where he played the suave diplomat speaking impeccable English and French and married to a fellow blue-blood, Maximiliane – 'Catsy' to her friends. But this playboy-cum-diplomat's real role was quite different: he was a key member of Hitler's spy unit, the Abwehr, and, despite being half Jewish, Maximiliane joined her husband in his efforts, often seducing their targets to encourage the flow of information. Sanary was just eight miles from Toulon, home of the French fleet, and the couple's budget for prising naval secrets was deep indeed. It was not long before Catsy had seduced her husband's tennis partner, the French naval officer Charles Coton. The husband and wife espionage duo were at play.

It might be assumed that with the establishment of the Abwehr as far back as the end of the Great War, it would be run and populated by the 'right sorts': well-born, well-educated and sophisticated old-school Germans with little in common with the chippy upstart Hitler. This was partly true, and why von Dincklage enjoyed his success building an effective spy network. He was undeniably attractive, in a louche way, and likeable and believable.

But from 1934 the Abwehr fell under the control of Joseph Goebbels who, at the age of 36, revelled in the sinister title of Reich Minister for Public Enlightenment and Propaganda. From that moment on, the Abwehr would work hand in hand with the Gestapo and SS. In the perversion that was life under the Nazis, when Hitler brought in the Nuremberg Laws, aimed at further isolating the Jewish population, the part-Jewish Catsy was declared 'fully Jewish' and no longer a German citizen. As 'good' Nazis, the couple had no option but to divorce, though they continued living together, most of the time, as well as enjoying numerous other lovers. Coco, now resident in a grand but gloomy wood-panelled suite at the Ritz, was among the baron's.

It is remarkable – and something of a bungle on the part of Goebbels – that the man running the Abwehr was Admiral Wilhelm Canaris. To his bosses he appeared to be an efficient Nazi spy chief; in fact whenever he could he tried, and succeeded, to rescue hundreds of Jews on their way to the camps and certain death. As the war wore on, he was regarded by Churchill as a vital asset to the Allies and one who could be trusted. Sir Stuart

Menzies, head of MI6 and Canaris' opposite number, also held him in great regard. Indeed, Menzies wrote in 1938: 'We know that Canaris is not a dyed-in-the-wool Nazi, but what might be termed a loyal officer or patriotic German.' Menzies also revealed that Churchill, not then in office, had spoken with the Abwehr chief, and it was Canaris who had persuaded Franco not to lead Spain into a joint Hispanic-German invasion of Gibraltar, a key naval base for the Allies. He was certainly not a saint, but he did instil certain standards in those he commanded; political assassination of enemies, for example, was strictly verboten.

The same could not be said of von Dincklage. He had been a confidant of Hitler as early as 1933 and, in his role in France, he sponsored anti-Semitic and pro-National Socialist propaganda in newspapers such as Paris Le Jour. He directly carried out Goebbels' orders and used encryption machines to contact Berlin. When his cover was blown by the French press, and he was exposed as a successful and active spy running a series of Nazi cells in the French capital, he went to Tunisia, an important French naval base, and resumed his activities. By then, of course, he had amassed a group of sympathetic French collaborators to the Nazi cause… not least of whom was Coco.

Tunisia was not his only port of call. Von Dincklage also spent time in Yugoslavia, regarded by Hitler as a potential problem and very much in the way of his 'grand plan' for Europe. In particular, the liberal King

Alexander was a target. Three months later, Alexander arrived in Marseilles for a state visit to France and was shot dead by a Bulgarian assassin. So too were his chauffeur and the French foreign minister. There seemed little doubt in the minds of the French and the British foreign secretary, Sir John Simon, that von Dincklage, acting on orders from Hitler, was directly responsible for the killings, which, like the Dallas assassination 29 years later of President Kennedy, was caught on film.

With von Dincklage now firmly out of town, Coco had taken up with designer and illustrator Paul Iribe. Together they launched a topical magazine which appealed to the ultra-nationalist Fascist mindset. Why ever not? She had the money; he had the talent; and she was falling in love with him. Then tragedy struck.

On a perfect Mediterranean afternoon in September 1935, Iribe collapsed while playing tennis at *La Pausa*, Coco's villa near Monte Carlo, financed by the Duke of Westminster. He had suffered a colossal heart attack and died in the ambulance aged 52. Coco was devastated. For the second time in 15 years she had lost a man with whom she was genuinely in love. Nothing could console her, not even her beloved narcotics. She found it impossible to concentrate on work and fled to London.

But when she finally began to emerge, she found herself once more in Toto's circle. She also attended Royal Ascot with Winston Churchill's son Randolph and was reacquainted with Churchill senior too. When back in Paris, Winston cabled her: *'I fear I shall not be free when*

I pass through on the tenth of December, but I shall be returning towards the end of January and look forward indeed to seeing you then.'

What strange and distorted times these were, and just where were Coco's true allegiances, other than to herself?

As Toto said to Laura Aitken:

'It might seem strange that Coco had lovers who were Nazis and such rabid anti-Semites at the same time as being friends with Winston Churchill and Randolph. But that's how it was before the war. Everyone hoped some arrangement could be made to stop Hitler from going further. Of course that never happened, and it was then that we all had to make up our minds about which side we were on. I knew quite a few German officers and, with few exceptions, they were smart, very civilised and charming. They weren't all monsters but, sadly, it only took a few monsters to start a war and bring about such unimaginable horrors. I should know. When all that became clear, that's when Coco should have turned her back on the Nazis. But no, she was too concerned with her own wealth to worry about what was right and wrong.'

CHAPTER 4

THE MAD, BAD, DANGEROUS TALLULAH

'I'm as pure as the driven slush, dah…ling.'
– Tallulah Bankhead

Every city has its so-called 'fast set', and Paris in 1932 seemed to produce a particularly good vintage unaffected by the Wall Street Crash and the resultant soup kitchens and suffering. The Beautiful People still had The Ritz, Maxim's, and the spectacularly avant-garde Monopole in Montmartre – the lesbian nightclub where beautiful women wearing Chanel and Schiaperelli were wooed by yet more beautiful women in tuxedoes and cropped hair, parted and oiled, none more infamous than the outrageous Miss Tallulah Bankhead.

So outrageous was Miss Tallulah, that she made her way into contemporary parlance as a verb: 'Tallulahing' was to dance, party and generally misbehave, preferably sexually. Indeed, the fast set often 'Tallulahed' the night away…

At 30, Bankhead was six years older than Toto, and not nearly as beautiful – few were – but at the peak of her social notoriety. Despite the absence of beauty, she was about as erotic as one could be without the censors, or certainly the chaste, reaching for the smelling salts. And when she purred her trademark 'Dah…ling', it was in a voice which the brilliant writer and actor Emlyn Williams described as 'steeped as deep in sex as the human voice can go without drowning.'

Both women were born into a privileged life – Tallulah's family was old Alabama aristocracy, courageously at odds with the accepted segregation of the Deep South; her grandfather and uncle were Democrat senators – though Tallulah's was short-lived. Her mother, aged just 21, died of sepsis three weeks after giving birth to her, and her distraught father, Will Bankhead, descended into alcoholic oblivion. As a young man he had tried acting, and the gene had certainly been passed on to his youngest daughter, who dabbled in Broadway (and excelled in exhibitionism). He finally lifted his head above the bottle and went into politics, like his forebears, becoming Speaker of the House under Roosevelt.

That December, 1932, Tallulah had starred in a plodding film drama, *Thunder Below*, which even her talents could not save, and was enjoying a break before returning to Broadway. When she spotted Toto at a society party she went straight over and introduced herself with the line she had first used in New York 12 years before: 'Hello, my name is Tallulah Bankhead and I'm a lesbian. What do you do?' It was used to astonish, and until this moment it always had; but Tallulah's reputation was an introduction all of its own, and Toto was neither surprised nor overly dazzled by the woman, just rather taken with her.

Toto and Tallulah became good friends and then lovers. Toto said of her: '*She was everything Coco was not. Totally mad, really, but always on the side of the angels. That's what attracted me to her.*'

Both were clever and worked ferociously hard. By 1933, Tallulah had featured in four films, while Toto was being photographed by principal photographers almost every day. Both had other lovers – men and women – and some they even shared, but they adored each other. Toto loved to see the various reactions when introduced to her outrageous friend, and Tallulah was thrilled to have such a beauty on her arm.

They were both politically liberal, too, and were worried about the way Europe was heading, feeling powerless against the march of Fascism. Toto, to her enormous cost, would find herself in over her head. Tallulah, however, was a friend of Eleanor Roosevelt, and 20 years later spoke vehemently against Senator Joseph McCarthy's Communist witch hunt. (She was credited with helping both Truman and Kennedy secure the presidency.) It would be difficult to identify anyone possessed of that sort of influence in the 21st century. Even the Madonna of her early days, or any one of the squawking puppet pop stars of today, would not be able to rival power like that…not to mention the ridiculous

Kardashians, who wouldn't qualify for the back runners, never mind the grid.

Tallulah was a woman of rampant appetites, lesbianism being just one of them, along with a taste for young men – too young in some cases. She once said: 'To deny me anything only inflames my desire.' She also said: 'When I left home for New York, my daddy told me to stay clear of alcohol and men. He didn't say anything about women and cocaine…' At a party in Manhattan, and refusing to drink any more of the port that always gave her a hangover, she requested cocaine instead. She failed to get it but, a week later, her request was met and therein began a close friendship with the white stuff. She was heard to say, 'Cocaine isn't habit forming; I should know, I've been taking it for years.

The British designer and socialite Nicky Haslam wrote harshly of his friend in The Spectator: 'Tallulah was a paradox, a good-time girl who never really had a good time; the life and soul, and often the death, of a party; a wisecracking spectre at the feast. She was too sharp, too overtly sexual, too self-indulgent, too knowing, too shocking – and she really was shocking – to be happy in her own skin.'

But Toto thought differently: *'Don't believe her critics, they were jealous hypocrites and Tallulah was living a life they would have lived if they had dared. She was very clever, funny and loved to shock. It was so amusing to see how people reacted to her. I was proud to be seen with her, though it was exhausting trying to keep up with her. For one thing, she never seemed to sleep and I needed my rest.'*

Unlike the Mdivanis, it would be unfair to say Tallulah was 'famous for being famous' because she had real talent, not just to amuse but as an actress. The trouble was, many of the parts she accepted were in scrawny turkeys of movies which would never get off the ground, whatever her effort. A move to the West End made a big difference, her fame as an actress assured with her performance as Amy in Sidney Howard's *They Knew What They Wanted*, which won the 1925 Pulitzer Prize for Drama.

But in her relentless quest to shock, Tallulah would often dispense with underwear while onstage or on a film set. While performing in Thornton Wilder's *The Skin of Our Teeth*, so many people in the audience complained that the actors' union Equity had to order her to wear knickers onstage. And when making Hitchcock's *Lifeboat*[11], her biographer Joel Lobenthal claims that nobody was sure if the matter should be 'referred to make-up or the hairdressing department'! Notwithstanding, the role of a journalist adrift in the Atlantic won her Best Actress of 1944 in the New York Critics' Circle awards.

One evening Toto and Tallulah were having dinner at Maxim's where, as a marketing ploy, the new owner had begun inviting the rich, famous and beautiful to dine. At a nearby table was Conrad Veidt, the German actor, who a year later would flee Germany with his new

---

[11] Tallulah's last line in *Lifeboat*, as a German ship steamed towards her, had an eerie portent: 'Some of my best friends are in the (concentration) camps…'

Jewish wife and settle in Britain. Tallulah had been trying to coax Toto into films, and there had been no resistance. Veidt, on being introduced, agreed to help. Two weeks later Toto was in London, testing for Alexander Korda.

Korda was a Hungarian-born director who was about to enjoy great success with *The Private Life of Henry VIII* and, in 1942, *The Third Man.* He was casting for *The Private Life of Don Juan* starring Douglas Fairbanks and the future Lady Korda, Merle Oberon. Toto landed the part of one of Don Juan's many mistresses, and the camera loved her, but Toto hated the monotony of movie making. It was not like modelling for a fashion shoot, which could stretch over a day but be fast and fun. Korda, like any other good director, would shoot every scene from many angles and lighting variations – fun for him, but not for Toto. 'How can you bear it?' she asked Tallulah. Later, Lady Deidre Curteis, who became a close friend of Toto in the 1950s, said: 'She hated the endless waiting between takes; she thought it was a form of imprisonment.'

Her appearances largely ended up on the cutting room floor and the film was a flop. Curiously, though her contract with Korda was terminated by mutual agreement, still shots of her were used to promote *Don Juan.* She was even interviewed by the press about the filming process. But the closest she got to the movies following that short foray was appearing at the London premiere of *Don Juan* with Tallulah. She and Korda remained friends, however.

Before Tallulah met Toto in Paris, she rather enjoyed motoring in her black Bentley, on Sundays, to Windsor…or, more specifically, to Eton College. Tallulah did not have any connection with Eton, so what was she up to? MI5, at the government's behest, was employed to investigate rumours that she had seduced six boys at the school, and so horrified were they by what they discovered that they ordered an inquiry by the Secret Service. The findings were kept under lock and key until 2000; but this is what the investigating officer, identified only as FHM, found:

'The charge against Miss Bankhead is quite simply a) that she is an extremely immoral woman and b) that in consequence of her association with some Eton boys last term, the latter had to leave Eton. She is both a lesbian and immoral with men…it is also said she 'kept' a negress in America before she came to the country in 1925, and she 'keeps' a girl in London now. As regards her more natural proclivities…she bestows her favours generously without payment.'

The report, handed to the then home secretary, the upright, teetotal moralist Sir William Joynson-Hicks, was vague about what went on between Tallulah and the boys – who no doubt could not believe their good fortune. But it is clear that she took them to the nearby Hotel de Paris on the banks of the Thames in Bray, a great favourite of the smart set. There she plied them with drugs (presumably cocaine) and drink and had sex with them, including acts that were described as 'indecent and unnatural'. Among the boys were said to be the grandson of the Earl of Rosslyn and the third son of Sir Matthew Wilson MP.

The school's headmaster, Dr Cyril Allington, a devout Christian and future Dean of Durham, did everything he could to cover up the scandal. As the agent FHM said: 'The headmaster is obviously not prepared to assist the enquiry…he wants to do everything possible to keep Eton out of the scandal.'

Had he co-operated, it is likely the Home Office would have ordered Bankhead to leave the country, never to return. As it was she went on to conquer London, often driving her Bentley behind a taxi hired solely for the purpose of leading the way so she didn't get lost! Among her many lovers in London were the politician Lord Birkenhead and his friend Lord Beaverbrook.[12]

Toto may have been promiscuous in so far as she had many lovers of both sexes, but she did not shout about it, and nobody thought her 'notorious'; whereas Tallulah ensured she was the very essence of it by shouting it from the rooftops. A fascinating portrait of Tallulah in later life was published in London's Daily Telegraph in 2000, just after the secret papers on the Eton scandal were released. The writer Robert Temple recounted meeting her in 1962 in New Jersey, when she was 65 and he 17. Temple had been working as a prop boy at a theatre, where she was soon to appear. She had

---

[12] Toto met Beaverbrook through Tallulah, and that encounter was to change her life forever.

apparently fallen out with the director, and Temple was deputed to calm her:

'I stayed with her for 48 hours. During that time we did not sleep… She had superhuman energy and went many nights without any sleep at all (the cocaine presumably) and had bourbon instead of blood in her veins. She devoured newspapers, she devoured books, she devoured people. She devoured penises (especially black ones), she devoured vaginas and breasts. She devoured life, life, life.

'Tallulah was totally uninhibited about nudity and without thought would strip down to her knickers and wander around with her breasts undulating. Tallulah's voracious sexual appetites were really 90 per cent for women, with only the occasional "black buck" thrown in for spice. The 1930s director Monty Banks told me wistfully that when he stayed next door to Tallulah's suite in a Paris hotel once, there was a genuine queue of beautiful girls waiting in the corridor to get into her bed. How could she do it? She worked her way through 15 girls in one night without a problem.'

Temple also recalled: 'Tallulah adopted me as her pet for some time. I befriended Robert Williams, her black chauffeur. Walking around in her knickers, Tallulah would make a detour into one of the bedrooms of her suite to have a quick bonk with Robert.'

And he concluded, rather more positively than Nicky Haslam: 'Tallulah was genuinely someone to be adored for her kindness and her generosity of spirit. She was intellectually brilliant, as witty as Oscar Wilde and a tribute to the vibrancy and radiance of the human spirit.'

No wonder Toto was fascinated by her mad, bad, dangerous friend, just as she had been by the phony Mdivanis.

CHAPTER 5

THE BRILLIANT, BRUTAL BEAVER

'…a strange attractive gnome, with an odour of genius about him.'

— Lady Diana Cooper

When Toto met the widowed Lord Beaverbrook the attraction was not physical, but one of curiosity. At 55, he was almost 30 years older than Toto, and had nothing of the classical good looks of Alexis Mdivani. At only five feet six inches, with small hands and feet and a large head, a very wide mouth and, to complete the caricature, a mole or wart (most certainly not a beauty spot) on his left cheek, he was the 'frog' to Mdivani's 'prince'. His raucous laugh was warm and infectious; it could also be menacing. He may have presented as an odd-looking specimen but, unlike the wretched charlatan Alexis, his title and his money were real. And he was powerful – stupendously so – and power, in his case, was the great aphrodisiac.

A school friend had once told Beaverbrook: 'God couldn't make your mouth any bigger without removing your ears,' hence the unflattering description of his resemblance to a frog.

She was also exhausted. The four-month dalliance with Tallulah – yes, it had lasted just four months – had suited them both. The two women appeared to be enjoying themselves, and seemingly didn't give a damn. But their moral compasses were not aligned. Tallulah was excessive in her habits: drugs, alcohol and sex, it really was a case of anything goes. Toto, by contrast, was aware of how her behaviour might have consequences; she had a conscience and she wanted to avoid hurting anyone.

William Maxwell Aitken was born in Ontario, Canada, in 1879, the fifth of 10 children. His father, the severe, grey-bearded Scottish Presbyterian minister, Rev William Cuthbert Aitken, and his wife Jane Noble were descended from tenant farmers. Aitken Junior (but he was always called Max) liked to describe a childhood spent in 'poverty', but it was all part of the rags-to-riches story he wove around himself. 'I am descended from a long line of agricultural labourers, going back to 1613,' he would say, 'therefore I feel quite equal to the Cecil family, except that none of my ancestors stole from church funds.' In fact, those 'agricultural labourers' – tenant farmers – did rather well economically. And the manse he was brought up in was a very large and attractive villa; indeed, one of the largest houses in the area and big enough for the Victorian-sized family and their servants, and now open to the public for conducted tours. True, there was no electricity or running water to begin with, but they soon had both, along with a telephone. There was nobody local to call, however, as the Aitkens had the only phone in town.

Max was a clever boy but, to the despair of his teachers, he took the view that classes were something of an optional extra and did not always attend. Instead, he had an early encounter with the press, selling newspapers on the street. Later, while working in a pharmacy as a teenager, he would jot down customers' gossip and sell it to his local paper, the St John Daily Sun…

That large head of his housed a very large brain, allied to a great deal of native cunning: Aitken realised he loved gossip; was drawn to it like a curtain twitcher to the neighbours; and it was this fascination with the minutiae of others' lives which underpinned much of his newspaper empire. He was, without a doubt, the inventor of the modern gossip column – in this case, The Daily Express's William Hickey, named after a little known 18th century Irish clergyman and writer.

Beaverbrook also had a natural gift for business, and by the age of 30 had made his first million (the equivalent of approximately $27 million today) from cement and banking, raising a few eyebrows from the Canadian stock exchange in the process. In fact, it was the question marks over his business dealings which persuaded Mr Max Aitken to visit England for the first time, in 1908, and to make it his home two years later.

His wealth, which amassed with every passing year, was used to buy his entrée into the upper classes who ran

Britain for the first half of the 20th century – a thing he relished, despite how much he said he despised them. (The feeling was mutual and remained so for much of his life) His social ambitions were helped by a knighthood in 1910, a baronetcy two years later, and ennoblement as Baron Beaverbrook in 1917. He married Gladys Drury, daughter of General Charles Drury CBE of the Canadian army, and his daughter Janet, a debutante, was presented on 1st May 1926 to the sphinx-like king and queen. (George V intensely disliked her father, as did Queen Mary, and had tried to block his baronetcy and later his peerage.)

It didn't matter that he was frowned on by the Establishment, he was buying his way in and cared not for their view that he was the distasteful *nouveau riche*. He behaved like an aristocrat, purchasing a large country estate, Cherkley Court near Leatherhead in the Surrey Hills, set in 400 acres at the top of a mile-long drive. There was also a fine London residence, Stornoway House by St James' Park, and a yacht, which he pronounced *yatt*, and later his own plane. He threw parties for hundreds of the right people, and Duke Ellington would be flown in as the entertainment. He employed an army of staff for his great houses, and had mistresses (by the dozen).

Friends referred to him as 'the Lord', though it may have been with a heavy dose of sarcasm. But that was preferable to George Orwell's description of him as 'a monkey on a stick'; and Cecil King (a Harmsworth family member) called his fellow newspaper owner 'an evil adventurer'…but coming from a man who tried to stage a coup in 1968 against the then prime minister, Harold Wilson, and install Lord Mountbatten as leader of an interim administration, one is tempted to acknowledge his name calling with a wry rise of an eyebrow. He was an enemy of Asquith and Baldwin, who famously said of his foe: 'Power without responsibility, the prerogative of the harlot throughout the ages.' Lord Salisbury called him 'a very wicked man'; Lady Diana Cooper, 'this strange attractive gnome with an odour of genius about him'; and Jane Portal, one of Winston Churchill's secretaries who had dealings with him during World War II, 'somebody you would instinctively walk away from.' His detractors queued up to relentlessly denounce him, it seemed: 'A vulgar Canadian'; 'a thumping crook'; 'tyrannous, vindictive and malicious'; 'an ironclad monster'…

Whatever the epithets, Beaverbrook was the supreme political fixer. He helped to unseat Herbert Asquith as prime minister so that his fellow Scots/Canadian Andrew Bonar Law would become leader of the Tory Party and, for eight months from 1922, British prime minister.

It is difficult to put into words just how powerful Beaverbrook was; and, as with an equal for Tallulah, there was no modern counterpart, not even Rupert Murdoch. To put this into context, the Daily Express was selling two and a half million copies a day, rising to more than four million within 30 years. There was no real competition, other than rival newspapers. There was no internet haemorrhaging news (and gossip) from screens, and no television doing the same, hosting desperate wannabees, has beens, and could-bees-again as an alternative to 24-hour news or programmes of cultural interest; it was just the BBC Home Service delivering dry and very formal daily news bulletins on the radio (or the wireless as it was known) by men with cut-glass accents wearing dinner suits (after 6pm), even though their listeners could not see them.

In 1922 Beaverbrook announced that the Daily Express stood for 'more life, more hope, more money, more work, more happiness. This is the creed to redeem Great Britain from the harsh aftermath of the war and set her on the path to prosperity', and Max was the impresario, the conductor of a great orchestra of writers who included, over the years, HG Wells, Bertrand Russell, Arnold Bennett and Harold Nicholson. His greatest friend in the literary firmament was the imperialist Rudyard Kipling, so much so that he named his younger son Peter Rudyard Aitken. Kipling was the only friend honoured in one very specific way: Beaverbrook hated staying anywhere except in one of his own (many) houses, but in the case of Kipling he made an exception as on several occasions he was an overnight guest at Batemans, Kipling's 17th century home in East Sussex. There is little doubt that Beaverbrook learned much from his friend, in particular this gem of advice: '*Write down your idea, put it away, look at it again and then delete every unnecessary word.*' That sums up the crisp way the Daily Express was written in its heyday.

There were some on the Express staff who were treated to favours beyond the dreams of colleagues, or rivals, and who, like their master, rarely came to the grand Art Deco office (later graced with a fine Oscar Nemon bronze head of their employer). All were personally recruited by 'the Beaver', not the editor.

For instance, Percy Hoskins was the Daily Express's chief crime reporter for decades, and the recipient of 55 Park Lane, paid for by his lordship… and where he was encouraged to run an open house for senior policemen. As a result, Hoskins wrote the most authoritative and exclusive stories on the world of the police and criminals.

Similarly, (Harry) Chapman Pincher, the doyen of 'scoop breakers', was given a flat in St James and a limitless expenses facility, which resulted in a ceaseless series of exclusive (and genuine) stories on defence and security issues gathered over oysters and sole at l'Ecu de France in Jermyn Street. Edward Heath, when prime minister, famously said after yet another of his front page revelations: 'Is there nothing we can do about Chapman Pincher?'

In the case of Carl Giles, the cartoonist, he never had to clear his work with the editor of either the Daily or Sunday Express where his drawings appeared, and was given the latest Bentley as his 'company car'.

Once they arrived at the Express office, Giles' brilliantly drawn cartoons were rigorously scrutinised by the Features department, because he had a habit of including details which were liable to shock more genteel readers. They were not exempt from slipping through the net on occasion, though, and his drawing of a workman with a condom hanging out of the back pocket of his overalls went unnoticed by the scrutineers…but not by the readers.

The newspaper's chief foreign affairs correspondent also enjoyed great privileges, and rightly so. Sefton Delmer was born in Berlin in 1904 of Australian heritage, and spoke only German until the age of five. After Oxford he joined the Express and became head of its Berlin bureau, in 1931 becoming the first British journalist to interview Adolf Hitler. He was suspected of supporting the Nazis, and simultaneously of being an agent of the British Secret Service, which was almost certainly the case, though it was never admitted. When in London, Beaverbrook put Delmer up in a suite at London's grand Grosvenor House hotel, and he would arrive at the Express clad in a sweeping black cape and trademark dark glasses, looking every inch the John Buchan spy.

During the war, Delmer played a vital role in the dark art of black propaganda with the political warfare executive, broadcasting to Germany in fluent German deriding Hitler and the impossibility of his vile cause. He was immediately placed on the Nazis' Most Wanted death list, but fortunately managed to evade any assassin. Toto and he would later cross paths, and it would radically change the direction of her life.

Essentially, Beaverbrook was the editor of every paper he owned through Express Newspapers, and he set the tone and the agenda, often dictating or commissioning articles and most days deciding the choice of the 'leaders' – the daily comment column. To put it bluntly: he decided for his readers the opinions they should have. The men (it was always men in those days) who bore the title of 'editor' were in the main remarkable, not least by having to learn, and learn quickly, how to handle the proprietor – or, as he was usually known, 'the principal reader'. In 1942, his unpredictable choice for the Evening Standard was Michael Foot, later the left-wing leader of the Labour Party and a great favourite of his patron. For a while Foot lived in close proximity in a grace-and-favour cottage on the Cherkley estate. In 2018, Ben McIntyre revealed in his brilliant book *The Spy and the Traitor* that Foot had been paid up to £50,000 by the KGB 'for information'. His master, with accidental wit, codenamed him 'Boot', the same name as Evelyn Waugh's – the nature notes correspondent of the Daily Beast in Scoop – reluctant hero. And the proprietor of the Beast? Lord Copper, modelled on none other than Lord Beaverbrook.

In 1954, Beaverbrook installed John Junor as editor of the Sunday Express, a unlikeable, Presbyterian Scot with a very long List of the Unacceptable – foremost of which were homosexuals – and, like his boss, a philandering hypocrite. Junor had been a Liberal parliamentary candidate for Kincardine in 1945, losing by just 642 votes, but life with the Beaver soon changed that. Within no time, Junor became a right-wing Tory of the old school, with friends to match, including the Rhodesian leader Ian Smith, Douglas Bader (the 'legless hero' of WW2), and most of the far reaches of the Conservative cabinet. Nonetheless, his eccentric product was a huge circulation success, and that made him a favourite of his paymaster: he too was given a cottage at Cherkley, and invited on holiday to the South of France.

On the other hand, Beaverbrook's most inspired choice as editor of the Daily Express was the brilliant and decent Liverpudlian Arthur Christiansen, who took over the helm aged 29 and stayed for 24 years. It was under 'Chris' that the paper sustained its relentless rise in sales, and he is still regarded as Fleet Street's greatest editor. His product was always optimistic and fun, yet never neglected to cover news and sport in great detail. It employed some of the finest writers of their generation, not least of whom was James Cameron, doyen of foreign correspondents. There were offices in Paris, Bonn, New York, Washington, Los Angeles and Moscow, and the vast staff in London was sent to every flashpoint in the world.

Beaverbrook was given to calling the Daily Express late in the evening, after his editor would have departed, and asking the senior journalist who picked up the phone: 'Who is in charge of the clattering train?' The line is from one of Churchill's favourite poems by Edwin

Milliken, and the answer, whether the proprietor knew it or not, was 'death'. But during World War II, it was not unusual for one of those senior men to answer the phone to find it was the prime minister calling. Churchill would ask what the front page 'splash' was, whereupon he would invariably suggest replacing it with another story relating to an event which, at that stage, nobody else knew about. Such was the power of Beaverbrook's Daily Express; and, as a result, such was the power of the man himself.

He enjoyed playing with people to see how far he could push them. In the 1950s, Harold Keeble, briefly editor of the Sunday Express before Junor, was invited for the weekend to Cherkley. On the first evening before dinner, this most agreeable of men was asked to join his host for a swim in the pool. 'After you, Mr Keeble,' – an order not a suggestion – was heard, at which the hapless Keeble dived into an almost frozen pool, the heating not having been turned on. 'How's the water, Mr Keeble?' he was then asked. The poor fellow, not wishing to offend, replied with teeth-a-chatter, 'Lovely, sir.' On jumping in and discovering the truth, Beaverbrook declared: 'Never lie to me, Mr Keeble. You're fired.' Which indeed he was. Until the following Tuesday.

Here was a man whose biographer (one of many, but one of the finest), the late Michael Davie, said: 'He had a lifelong dread of dullness, which conditioned his life as well as his papers; his instinctive belief in personality as the clue to history and current events; his exceptional memory, especially for financial and sexual scandal; and his keen interest in gossip…' He might have added that he had to dictate not only every article, but every relationship too. His devoted daughter Janet remembers finally persuading him to come to lunch at the farm in Somerset he had bought for her. She went to great lengths to arrange lunch and was thrilled that she could show off the improvements she had made to the place. In the event, he sat on the terrace eating sandwiches he had brought with him, refusing to socialise. 'It was,' said Janet, 'his way of showing who was boss.' Similar stories were told by editors after receiving early morning phone calls berating them for some perceived fault in that day's edition. Accompanying the Beaver's admonishment could be heard a female, giggling: the whole show had been staged to prove to both the editor, and whoever had been in bed with the proprietor the night before, that he was to be revered, and feared.

Fabulously rich, at times and in equal measure sentimental, cold and ruthless, Beaverbrook was a capricious and bitter enemy to have. He was given to generosity and meanness, cruelty and thoughtfulness, and it was into this maelstrom of a man's world that Toto, not yet 26 and a year younger than Janet, was about to enter. Toto's life in Paris had been populated by a cast of the beautiful and the rich who spent their days and nights at play, hedonists each one, at some level or other. But none of them was remotely powerful or had the sort of influence her new lover did – for, bizarrely, they did become lovers.

As Toto would soon learn, Beaverbrook was a complex character, devious and always mischievous. He could be greatly feared – reputations were created and just as quickly annihilated on the fancy of the Beaver – and yet be in fear himself. In the early days of commercial passenger flight he would sing Psalm 23, loudly – '*The LORD is my shepherd […] he maketh me to lie down in green pastures…*' – on take-off and touchdown. Evelyn Waugh, when asked if he believed in the devil, replied, 'Of course, how else could you account for Lord Beaverbrook?' Even his great friend Churchill called him 'Machiavelli'. And Enoch Powell, Greek scholar, wartime officer and right-wing MP, went further: 'He was a most evil man.'

Whatever they all thought, the man himself was in no doubt: 'I am on the side of the Little Pig against the Big Bad Wolf.' He made no mention of the consequences when *he* was the Big Bad Wolf.

Michael Foot remembers being inducted into The Circle at Cherkley, where Beaverbrook would preside over dinner from the head of a long table. From 1947, and from the head of that table, Beaverbrook would look out of a window that faced a large wooden cross, erected in the garden to commemorate the death of his son Peter, godson of Kipling, who was killed in a boating accident in Sweden. Foot recalls: 'The assorted company, the polemical free-for-all, the deluge of drink and journalism and politics, the orangutan manner, the absolute rule that no holds were barred; indeed customarily, an incitement from the host that the more eminent his guests, the more ferocious should be the cross examination.'

Beaverbrook's dinner parties were rowdy affairs, with arguments, usually political, fuelled by wine, and more wine; and the more the wine, the louder the debate. Foot recalls Toto being at those dinners in the 1930s: 'An exquisitely beautiful girl sat at my side, at ease, who the following day was floating through the house, her disturbing presence everywhere.'

Then, another ritual: the host would lead his guests across the hall, down four steps and into a small cinema. Without exception, the assembly would have to watch his favourite film, *Destry Rides Again*, a better than average Western starring Marlene Dietrich and James Stewart. Invariably, Beaverbrook would doze off...the cue for some guests to follow suit. Toto usually excused herself. She preferred her heroine, Pauline, from that first flickering silent movie she saw in Java.

She said: *'People said the most terrible things about Max, but what struck me was his intelligence, instinct and energy. He loved to entertain and show off, but not in a bad way. He educated me during our time together; I was in my twenties yet sitting down with prime ministers and presidents who were treating me on more or less on equal terms.'*

When Beaverbrook and Toto met, the old man soon became immensely fond of her, just as he was of Jean

Norton[13] – he was already one of the richest self-made men in Britain. She discovered he was a former (and somewhat reluctant) Conservative MP for Ashton-Under-Lyne, and a member of the Lloyd George coalition cabinet during the Great War in the role of Minister of Information (for which read 'propaganda'...), a post perfectly suited to his talents. He was a remote and disagreeable father who could, at times, also be very loving. Certainly Janet, the eldest child and only daughter, seemed to adore him.

Through his newspapers, the Daily Express, the Sunday Express and the London Evening Standard, Beaverbrook helped plot the direction of British politics. And though he insisted the content struck the proverbial 'high moral tone' – somewhat at odds with his own life – he relished the gossip of the moment. He claimed to have kept the Puritan Presbyterian faith of his childhood, yet behaved appallingly towards women. He bullied and charmed; he destroyed and built up.

Peter Masefield, who worked with Beaverbrook during World War II, observed: 'For all his foibles and tough exterior, he was at heart deeply sensitive and often lonely...kind and generous, but also hasty and vindictive.' He suffered badly from asthma, and had terrible bouts of depression, his worst in 1918 at the end of the war. As

---

[13] During the General Strike, which sent whole swatches of the country into very real poverty, the extent of which was truly shocking, Gladys, Beaverbrook's wife, and two of his legion of mistresses, Edwina Mountbatten and Jean Norton, worked on the Express switchboard and in the canteen. Edwina later admitted that it was the first time she had ever been in a kitchen.

a cabinet minister, he felt an acute responsibility and was heard to say: 'A million British lives lost, the flower of a generation…'

Toto was not put off by her early encounters with this strangely charismatic, gnome-like frog-face of a man. But this was the one relationship he could not dictate.

CHAPTER 6

A VERY ODD COUPLE

'I have been blessed with [...] the ability to recall without having to refer to notes.
This was something Max had too.'

— Toto

Different worlds they may well have inhabited, but Toto and Beaverbrook had one thing in common: the barefaced promiscuity that defined the upper classes in the 1930s. The 'free-love' of the 1960s seems positively virginal when compared to what played out in grand country houses and the mansions of Mayfair, and personified by the then Prince of Wales, the future (uncrowned) king. Depending on 'the Lord's' whim, many of those affairs — other than his own, of course — were reported in his newspapers, often as not because Beaverbrook himself would ring one of his senior journalists, almost on a daily basis, with the low-down on who had been doing what and to whom. He was also prone to calling the William Hickey editor asking for the veracity of that morning's story on some public figure or other. On being assured it was correct in every detail, he would reply: 'Good, I'm having dinner with them this evening.'

The Hickey column chronicling these scandals was the invention of the proprietor, and Tom Driberg[14], future Labour MP and well-known homosexual – and later rumoured to have been a Soviet spy – was installed as its editor. By the 1960s, the volume of scandals reported was such that the unofficial motto of Hickey was 'Their despair is our delight!' It was the treacherous Driberg who persuaded Beaverbrook to let him write his biography, and that both the Sunday and Daily Express should serialise it for payment of £120,000 (in today's values). When the finished manuscript was read for libel by Helenus Milmo QC, acting for the publisher Weidenfeld and Nicholson, his written opinion was: 'Driberg portrays you as an unprincipled adventurer, evil and spiteful, devoid of all loyalties, consumed with lust for power.' Detractors would no doubt have said 'Spot on.' After numerous cuts were made, the serialisation went ahead. What readers made of it over their toast and marmalade remains a mystery.

Beaverbrook, like many a powerful genius before and since, had a huge sexual appetite, perhaps semi-sated by his affair with Tallulah. But this affair of all others was the one which worried his daughter Janet the most. Max

---

[14] Driberg was once caught fellating another man, and when asked by the policeman for his name gave it as 'William Hickey'. A case was never brought.

was going through his 'actress period', as she called it – and by that she meant a phase of engaging 'flighty, tarty, on-the-make types'. There was one furious row, by all accounts, between father and daughter because of the outrageous, shameless Tallulah. Beaverbrook had told Janet that it was time she 'stopped gadding about' and that she should 'develop a sense of responsibility'. The furious reply: 'Responsibility? To whom? Mother? What about you!' With that she grabbed a valuable Chinese vase, and smashed it on the floor.

Beaverbrook would meet his political and business cronies, and his increasingly long and complicated line of mistresses – many of them the wives of the cronies – at the grand Stornoway House, complete with ballroom. When Toto met the Beaver, he had been a widower for seven years and had enjoyed innumerable lovers, including some of the greatest beauties of the day. (One can assume they were not drawn by his non-resemblance to Rudolph Valentino but by his power, his influence, and his almost bottomless money pot.) 'He was,' said his granddaughter Lady Jeanne Campbell in a 1996 television documentary, 'able to do anything, to arrange anything. He was like a monsoon, he brought chaos, disorder and life. It's a Presbyterian thing; he shouldn't have mistresses so he'd have the mistresses, and then be terrified he was doing the wrong thing and treat them badly.' Laura describes him as 'stimulating, primitive and almost wicked'.

As part of the rebellion against his father's Knoxian strictures, he enlisted as lovers (in addition to Tallulah),

Lady (Edwina) Mountbatten, yet to be Vicereine of India and possibly the most promiscuous women of her day, and the pianist Harriet Cohen, later a champion of the refugees from Nazism. Others on the inexhaustible list were Rebecca West, the novelist and wife of HG Wells, and Doris Delevingne, who rose from a lowly start as a suburban haberdasher's daughter to lover of assorted millionaires, including Prince George of Kent, the bisexual son of King George V. She later married the rounded and balding Viscount Castlerosse. More of these two later.

The woman who really was known as his mistress – as in long term – was Jean Norton who, like Tallulah, was his lover before Gladys, the first Lady Beaverbrook and mother of his three children, died from a brain tumour in 1927. Jean Norton was married to the future Lord Grantley, a film producer who had been badly wounded in the World War I. Grantley was aware of his wife's arrangement with his friend Beaverbrook. Jean stayed with Beaverbrook for 20 years in a house on the Cherkley estate…at the same time as his other carnal cavortings were being conducted.

Those of us raised in the post-war era might find it impossible to comprehend a life of such debauchery. Vaguely familiar as they might have been about unpleasant bouts of gonorrhoea amongst the lower classes, or the deadly seriousness of syphilis, they were not living with the fear of AIDS and HIV – and were certainly not living by middle- and working-class morals of the time, whatever shape or form they took.

As we've noted, it was his fling with Tallulah that concerned Janet the most: 'Father seemed to be getting too fond of Tallulah, and I couldn't bear the thought of him getting hurt. When I told him so he was defiant, telling me to shut up and mind my own business. Looking back, it was as if he was, for a while, in line with Tallulah's own creed; flying in the face of every conventional morality.'

When Lady Beaverbrook was dying, he sent her this note: 'How I wish you were well again. There is so much happiness in life for you and me if you will get strong.' Were these the words of a man deeply regretting his behaviour? More likely, he was able to square it with the fact that now he was rich and upper class, he would act the part. When she died he finally returned from Biarritz. He confessed to Janet: 'She was my harbour. I loved her so much, but she was too good for me.'

His affair with Jean Norton had begun a year before her death, and Gladys liked her, despite her being the third – even fourth, or tenth – member of their marriage. And compared with most, with the obvious exception of Mrs Norton and Harriet Cohen, Toto's affair with Beaverbrook was comparatively lengthy at 10 months. The difference between Toto and the others was her interest and active participation in the great political issues of the day, which were keeping Max very busy. Indeed, despite her hob-knobbing with Paris' high society, she had developed a keen nose for politics and was anxious about the way Europe appeared to be heading. She was no vacuous beauty – or in today's language, an 'airhead' – and she was about to learn at the Beaver's little feet.

Beaverbrook had never been scared of a fight; on the contrary, it seemed to be what he owed his very existence to. He had already lost his battle with three-times prime minister Stanley Baldwin and the Conservative Party over his beloved Empire Free Trade Crusade[15] – the reason, incidentally, why the two Express titles to this day, more than 40 years after they passed from the Beaverbrook family's hands, still wear the Crusader motif on their mastheads – but that did not mean there would not be other windmills for tilting. One of them – surprising, considering his legion of aristocratic friends – was the English upper class. His new chums, Aneurin Bevan, the Welsh Labour politician, and Churchill's acolyte Brendan Bracken, the Irish journalist who memorably called Bevan a 'Bollinger Bolshevik' (a reference the Socialist's prodigious intake of champagne), were happy to join this particular crusade. One of his more unlikely friends, and great friends they were, was the great Irish nationalist Tim Healy, who the Beaver's daughter Janet adored. Her father's affection for Healy even stretched to his eventual recognition of Ireland's right to be independent. Maybe it was an example of Max being contrary for its own

---

[15] Beaverbrook founded the Empire Free Trade Crusade party to fight for free trade and fiscal union within all countries of the British Empire, with stiff barriers to goods from other trade blocks outside the empire. One MP was elected, but by the end of the '30s there were more pressing concerns for the Beaver.

sake…just as he would insist his editors joined him for a walk in one of London's grand royal parks, during which he would regularly relieve himself against a tree.

Beaverbrook was an isolationist and believed (thus, therefore, did his newspapers assert) that Britain and the empire should not be getting involved in other nations' problems – were he alive today, he would single-handedly have led the exit from Europe! – but developments in Germany in the mid-1930s were threatening to destabilise his policy of isolation. At first, he had some sympathy for Adolf Hitler and his National Socialist Party; indeed, he watched with approval as Hitler took a firm hand where it was badly needed in his country, and he approved his pledge that Germany would leave the League of Nations, one of Max's bête noires. But all that changed with the Night of the Long Knives, when the true brutality of the Nazis showed in terrible bloody technicolour. The murder of Hitler's rival Ernst Rohm and his followers made up Beaverbrook's mind, and his editors were instructed accordingly. It also drew both him and Churchill towards Stalin's Russia, and he became great friends with the Soviet ambassador to Britain, Ivan Maisky. It may well have been an understanding based on the old saying 'your enemy's enemy…' He was proved right.

It was rather useful, then, that Toto spoke fluent and barely accented French, German and Italian, along with her Dutch and English. She also loved opera – a taste her lover never developed – and these two passions would be put to excellent use.

Neither Toto nor Max was in a monogamous relationship, though Toto tried, not always successfully, to be discreet. Throughout the 1930s she was pursued by the Prince of Wales (unsuccessfully), Lord Castlerosse, despite him owing his livelihood to Max, and Randolph Churchill, son of Beaverbrook's closest friend Winston. The affair with Valentine Castlerosse was such that his wife threatened him with divorce proceedings, naming Toto as co-respondent. But it was the affair with Randolph which would have the most lasting impact.

Late in 1934, Beaverbrook was invited, along with Toto, to a dinner hosted by Sir Robert Vansittart, permanent under-secretary at the Foreign Office. A fellow guest was the Italian ambassador to London, Count Dino Grandi, who was happy to invite the most influential newspaper proprietor in Britain to meet the Italian leader Benito Mussolini. This invitation was duly taken up by the Beaver, and in early 1935 he took Toto with him to Rome, together with Sefton Delmar, the highly regarded chief foreign affairs correspondent of the Daily Express. In the event, although he found Mussolini 'amusing' (as in laughable), and Delmar got an interview, Mussolini failed to win over Beaverbrook as a supporter.

As Toto recalls: '*I thought Mussolini was a ridiculous, comical figure, little did I know what damage and hatred he would bring to his country.*' She stayed on for the opera in Rome, and at La Scala in Milan…and began to observe the newly fascist Italy first hand. On her return, she and

Beaverbrook discussed how best her beauty, sharp mind, linguistic skills and political interests could be put to use. It was agreed: she would become, to all intents and purposes, a British agent; or, more accurately at that time, a Beaverbrook agent. *'I have been blessed with a great memory,'* she added, *'the ability to recall without having to refer to notes. This was something Max had too.'* Beaver had other traits, however: extraordinary powers of concentration (when it suited him), an infinite memory, and a deep streak of paranoia. He often instructed his very own reporters to bring him information on the activities of his enemies, real and imaginary. He also had spies, mostly amateurs, keeping an eye on his wife, and his lovers, and even his children. On one occasion he received a telegram from Doris Delevingne (Lady Castlerosse), who was spying on Toto whilst she was away from Beaverbrook's side*:*

'To Lord Beaverbrook, Stornoway House, St. James's, London: Toto Koopman in Paris fumbled silly by Allen Paulas's brother-in-law. He is frightful but rich. They are travelling together. More if needed. Love, Doris Castlerosse. Grand Hotel, Venice.'

But with Toto it was different, as she would spy *for* him, in order to keep him fully informed on ominous developments in Europe. News then deemed worthy of dissemination would appear in one of his newspapers and would be passed on to Churchill or his friends in government.

In one of her solo trips to Rome, Toto learned that

Mussolini was determined to win back territory in Africa which had once been part of the Roman Empire. This would – and by October of 1935 did – involve invading Abyssinia (Ethiopia), using poison gas in the process. Apart from an exclusive story forecasting the move in the Daily Express, there was little the Beaver could do except to ensure his newspapers championed the Emperor of Abyssinia, Haile Selassie, as 'the 'Lion of Judah': the little man standing up to the Italian bully. But it was a disturbing sign of where Europe was heading…

As it happened Toto, through the Beaver, had met Stewart Menzies, soon to be 'C', as the head of MI6 was known, and Ian Fleming's model for 'M' in his James Bond adventures. She also ran into Fleming who, despite his aristocratic background and dashing looks, she found 'intensely boring'. Fleming was from the eponymous banking family, and Menzies came from a hugely wealthy family with shipping and whisky interests, and was, it was rumoured, falsely, to be the son of King Edward VII. When Menzies and Toto met, the Old Etonian was deputy to the head of MI6, Admiral Hugh Sinclair, whom he succeeded in 1939. Toto was now riveted by espionage, in all of its guises, and though his position meant he was unable to share too many details of the service with her, he encouraged her to look and listen – most particularly to listen – while on her travels.

Toto Koopman soon left for Berlin and the State Opera House for a season of Strauss, under the Austrian conductor Clemens Krauss, who had taken charge after

the sackings of all leading Jewish musicians. But it was
no ordinary trip.

CHAPTER 7

THE VISCOUNT AND OTHER LOVERS

'Valentine, it's Randolph. Guess where I am? I'm in bed with your wife!'

— Randolph Churchill

As we've noted, neither Toto nor Beaverbrook maintained monogamous relationships, and one of Toto's more successful pursuers was Valentine Browne, Viscount Castlerosse, heir to the earldom of Kenmare. Castlerosse owed his enjoyment of the good life entirely to the current lover of the woman he desired so much, for it was Beaverbrook who employed him both as a director of his three newspapers and as the writer of Londoner's Log, the gossip column on the Sunday Express, recognised as essential reading by the paper's more socially ambitious subscribers.

He was rarely away from the Beaver's side (with the exception of the times he was in Toto's bed), because his patron viewed him as much court jester as journalist. He was a fixture at almost every Cherkley dinner party, where he indulged his other passions: fine food, in copious quantities, and drink, in copious quantities. The affair with Valentine Castlerosse was, as we've said, such that his wife threatened him with divorce proceedings, naming Toto as co-respondent. But it was his wife who, in time, would become better known…

Doris Delevingne, sender of that telegram from Venice 'telling tales' on Toto, married Castlerosse in 1928, and it was her first step up the ladder (the first rung being born the daughter of the lower middle-class). Her ambitions knew no bounds; neither did her promiscuity. In short, she was a courtesan, and it was she who, according to papers released in 2018, had an affair with Winston Churchill in the 1930s. The source of the story was Churchill's private secretary, Jock Colville, in an interview he gave in 1985 to archivists at Churchill College, Cambridge, and kept under lock and key for 33 years.

The alleged affair lasted three years, from 1933 to 1936, but was a very on-off business, conducted mostly when Churchill was in the South of France during his so-called 'Wilderness Years'. Whether it really happened is open to much debate, but the circumstantial evidence is strong enough and strengthened by the interview with Colville who said: 'He certainly had an affair with her…a brief affair.' To intrigue us further, in 1942 Churchill, by then prime minister, intervened to get Doris back from New York to London, where she decamped to the Dorchester, accompanied by a portrait of her by

Winston. When she killed herself in her room shortly after her homecoming, Churchill was desperate to get hold of the painting, lest it led to questions about their relationship. There was only one man he could rely on to succeed in the task: Beaverbrook. He did not let his great friend down.

What is certain is that Doris Delevingne had an affair with another Churchill, Winston's son Randolph, who was also one of Toto's lovers, and who would prove to be a great friend and support when war had dealt her a near-lethal blow.

Janet Kidd, the Beaver's daughter, with much delight, recounted a story about the deeply unattractive Valentine Castlerosse. Asleep in his hotel bedroom in New York, he accepted a reverse-charge call from London. It was Randolph Churchill, who stated: 'Valentine, it's Randolph. Guess where I am? I'm bed with your wife!' It seems the shameless incestuousness of the upper classes knew no bounds.

Churchill junior was three years younger than Toto and despite, or more probably because of, his famous father, he never quite made a success of anything. At Eton he was lazy and unpopular, and subject to beatings by other boys. When not at school, he was encouraged to attend his father's dinner parties and have an opinion on the issues being debated around the table. This gave him a considerable taste for alcohol, which was indulged by Winston. By the age of 18 he was drinking brandy heavily, and he became an uncouth, crashing bore when drunk. He then dropped out of Oxford, after just a year.

But despite the slow start, as a young man – he was just 20 – Randolph set sail for the US, where he embarked on a lecture tour which earned him a remarkable amount of money – £140,000 in today's values.

On his return, he shared a house in London with John Betjeman, became a journalist, ran a chauffeur-driven Bentley and gambled heavily, and badly, and had to be bailed out (constantly) by his parents. But he wrote well, and often, for a variety of newspapers, including those owned by Beaverbrook and Max's friend and rival Lord Rothermere. He also became MP for Preston during the war, during which he served as a major in the 4th Hussars. When he met Toto he was a good-looking young man and, when sober, reasonable company. But it was his close friend, Beaverbrook's son Max, who was about to make the biggest impact.

CHAPTER 8

KEEPING IT IN THE FAMILY

'Five years of you and I still miss you. It is rather a nice thought…'

– Toto

When Toto returned from her solo trip to Munich in 1935 it was with disquieting news, so from Croydon aerodrome she made straight for Cherkley to talk to Beaverbrook. Compulsory military service was about to be introduced in Germany as the arms build-up intensified. She had heard that only Aryans could serve, and that those called up, or already serving, must marry other Aryans. Which posed the obvious question: What would be the fate of Jews already in the forces?[16]

The Beaver and she were talking in his study, along with his great friend and director of the Evening Standard,

---

[16] The answer became clear 50 years later: Hitler apparently vetted every one of them and they were allowed to stay, some serving in the highest ranks.

the wealthy, one-eyed Mike Wardell[17], when there was a light knock at the door. In walked a tall, dashing – a 'blade' as such was referred to in the '30s – young man in his mid-20s. His name was John William Maxwell Aitken, and the first man Toto felt she would very much like to fall in love with. But herein lay a problem: this dashing young man's father was her current lover; Father had just introduced son to mistress…

Max Aitken, like his father, was born in Canada – in Montreal – in 1910, the year the family moved permanently to London. As a father to Max, Peter and Janet, Beaverbrook was busy, mostly disinterested, and distinctly absent, taking the Edwardian view that the rearing of children was the prerogative of mothers – and nannies and governesses, all of whom could be afforded and were hired. Max was brought up in Cherkley, which his father had just bought, and the first nanny he remembered, for all the wrong reasons, was a Miss Gulch, Wicked Witch of the East figure, known to her charges as 'the Brute'. Other staff consisted of Rennie, the imperious butler, two footmen in green livery and white gloves, a chef, three kitchen maids, four housemaids, gardeners, grooms and two chauffeurs and, finally, Miss Evans the housekeeper. After the dreaded Brute suddenly and inexplicably disappeared, Ada Krelle, a German governess, arrived – a vast improvement on her predecessor.

---

[17] Like many before, and after him, a some-time lover of Tallulah Bankhead.

The children were used to lots of guests, the likes of Asquith, Bonar Law and Rudyard Kipling. Winston Churchill's visits delighted the three young Aitkens the most, however, as he was the dispenser of paper bags of fruit drops.

When the time came for the children to be sent to their boarding schools, it was Westminster for Max, where he excelled at football, the school's main winter sport. Westminster was everything Cherkley was not, and he grew up fast when he was there, and forged some good friendships as he did. As a result, when he moved to Pembroke College, Cambridge, he was immensely popular, and gained a Blue for soccer and golf, which he played off scratch. He was also a fine and competitive tennis player. He then joined the University Air Corps and gained his pilot's licence. When he came down from Cambridge, Max joined the Auxiliary Air Service and spent his weekends flying a variety of aircraft and, for the first time, mixing with men from all corners of the country, and all classes.

So the 25-year-old Max – 'Little Max' as he was known in the family; ironic, given he grew much taller than his father – whom Toto first encountered was a cultured, sporty, good-looking pilot…and the absolute opposite of his famous father. In the words of John Junor, Max was 'handsome beyond measure, chased by every good-looking girl in London.' The only thing father and son had in common, in fact, other than their name, was the Express, where Max had been installed as a (frequently absent) junior manager in his father's hopes that he would one day succeed him. Any thoughts of the Express were utterly eclipsed, however, when Max sat down and listened, with growing fascination, to what Toto had to say about Munich. He knew Toto was his father's mistress, but hadn't met her until now. Her staggering beauty captivated him but so too did her faultless abilities as a reporter of current events, and the fearlessness which went with it. Max was staying the night at Cherkley and, later, when his father was on one of his interminable transatlantic telephone calls, he asked Toto to walk with him in the garden.

Max was living in a small flat in Oakley Street, Chelsea, owned by the Express group. It was neither luxurious nor spacious, but it was private…or at least it became so when Max asked friends not to drop round unannounced. A month of clandestine meetings with Toto passed without alarm, which was remarkable considering the network of snoopers Beaverbrook employed; but then, by complete coincidence, Baroness Budberg, friend of Beaverbrook and mentor to Toto, was in the back of a taxi in Sloane Square when she spotted the young lovers walking out of the Royal Court Theatre. Moura Budberg was well versed in the forming of fast judgments about people in her role as a British agent – in fact she is thought to have been a double agent, spying also for the Russian secret service, the OPGU – and it was clear to her that this was no casual meeting of two people who had just been introduced.

The following morning Budberg rang Stornoway House to make an appointment to see Beaverbrook. When he heard her news, the man was apoplectic – despite his numerous infidelities, he strongly disapproved of Toto's – and summoned Toto, who was in the Ritz having lunch with her brother Ody.[18] One doesn't need to be a Puritan to understand why Beaverbrook was quite so enraged, and when she eventually walked into Stornoway House he let rip, calling her a whore and a 'bloody negress' – to which she apparently laughed loudly, which only fuelled his fury. He then pleaded with her to stop seeing his son and, when she refused, he resorted to threats of vengeance.

At first, he considered ordering his newspapers to run articles denouncing her – what is now known as a 'hatchet job' – but on closer examination he realised that, by association, he could emerge from that as muddied as her. Instead, he issued a blanket ban on any coverage of Toto, declaring: 'I never want that woman's name or photograph ever to appear in my papers again. *Do I make myself clear?*'

Max was at the grand Art Deco Express building when he received his father's call. He immediately took the short taxi ride from Fleet Street to St James's. But much of Beaverbrook's wrath had been exhausted in his confrontation with Toto, and now he dropped into

---

[18] By now a successful tennis player and member of the Dutch Davis Cup team, and who was pleased his little sister was finally with someone of her own age and whom she seemed to love.

'hurt and disappointed father' mode, thinking that Max would apologise profusely…and move on. How little he knew his son. Max stood his ground, and despite saying sorry if he'd 'upset the old man' then rubbed salt into his umbrage by telling him how much he loved Toto and wanted to marry her. Beaverbrook was used to moving from one mistress to another, and having mistresses move on to another lover or another, and had it been any other man, he probably would have accepted the situation as par for the course. But his son? And the mention of love? And *marriage*? To have Toto – that negress – as his daughter-in-law? *Out of the question.*

In fairness to Beaverbrook, it must have been one of the most humiliating events of his tempestuous life. He was a man used to getting his own way, always, and dictating how those who knew him, and especially his family, should behave. Consequently, the two men had an explosive falling out, which resulted in Max being sacked from the Express, being cut off financially, and being disinherited. The company flat in Oakley Street was not mentioned, however, and Max certainly wasn't going to remind his father of it.

Few doubted that Beaverbrook was unusually fond of Toto, and she of him; but what he failed to grasp was that his son and Toto really were in love.

Max and Toto met at the Oakley Street flat. Though his source of income had disappeared overnight, there was enough money in both of their accounts to allow them to live very much in the style to which they were used. He would get a job flying, they decided; something he was far better at and more interested in than his father's bloody newspapers. Toto, they knew, could go back to modelling at any time, though not for any of the fashion pages in the Express stable… By late evening the couple had worked out their immediate future together – or at least Toto thought they had. But Max had other ideas and, on bended knee, the Honourable Max Aitken proposed marriage to Miss Catharina Koopman. And, in spite of what she had always said about never wanting to marry or have children, she accepted.

By way of retaliation, Beaverbrook embarked on a campaign to have the couple – Toto, in particular – ostracised in London society. '*He turned very nasty. He called me "that black bitch"*,' she recalled. He told anyone who would listen that she was 'a slut, a common prostitute' and 'totally without morals' and that she 'would go to bed with anyone, male or female'. In fact, bisexuality aside, she was behaving just like him! Those who listened, unless they were reliant on Beaverbrook for income or patronage, saw the hypocrisy crystal-clear, and there was very little falling off in the number of invitations coming the couple's way, and their mantelpiece displayed a regular succession of embossed cards.

Max and Toto were unfazed by Beaverbrook's 'campaign', and decided to holiday away from the spotlight. They went to Spain, to a place near Barcelona, with the celebrated Josep Maria Sert and his wife Isabella Roussadana, one of the phoney 'marrying Mdivani' gold-digging family who courted tragedy as efficiently as they did other people's fortunes. Isabella, known as Roussy, knew Toto from her Paris days and had married Sert, aged 55, when she was just 19, displacing his former wife – and her friend – Misia. The couple were not to Max's taste, but he stuck it out for three weeks, exploring the Catalonian capital, sailing, and enjoying time away from his father's fury. Indeed, he felt it best to lay low and see how things played out.

They also went to Switzerland, on a most peculiar trip. Max's sister Janet had divorced her first husband, the gambling addict Ian Campbell (later Duke of Argyll) who stole her jewels while the couple were on honeymoon. That year she'd married Drogo Montagu, son of the Earl of Sandwich who, happily, did not turn out to have kleptomania, and Max and Toto were invited to join them on their honeymoon. Janet Kidd, of that first strange night, relates in her splendid autobiography *The Beaverbrook Girl*: 'We arrived at the hotel and caught our first glimpse of the rich and beautiful people staying there. I stole an apprehensive glance at Toto. She was outstandingly attractive, having been ditched by Alexander Korda, Valentine Castlerosse and father in turn, yet arrived on Max's doorstep with no trace of mental or physical wear and tear.'

It is clear Janet did not have the full facts. Toto was 'ditched' by Beaverbrook only when she fell in love with his son, there is no evidence of an affair with Korda, and as for being ditched by the overweight Castlerosse...well, he should be so lucky!

Janet continues: 'Apart from her devastating good looks, Toto was quiet, shy and a very nice person who had come to love Max deeply. I believe that Max felt the same about her.' She added this sad note: 'To be Eurasian in 1935 and expect society to take you seriously was like crying for the moon. Society had yet to grow up.'

But back to the night's strange events: 'Our honeymoon night was like something out of a French farce. Both Toto and I had gone to bed tired after our long journey and the champagne we had consumed en route. We expected our men and, in my case, my brand new husband, to put in an appearance after "one last nightcap" in the bar. Two hours later, Drogo was still missing. There had been times like this before at parties. I would find him upstairs with a girl or in the car park, the summerhouse, somewhere, looking rather flushed. He would greet me with "Thank God you came Jan" as I led him meekly away.'

And more: 'This time we searched the bar, lounge, dining room, dance floor, card room, billiard room, garden and terrace without success. Only the bedrooms remained. I found the suite he was in and it was booked in the name of Baroness von Thyssen. I tapped discreetly on her door. "Drogo?" My tone was soft and honey-sweet. From inside came a sudden urgency of whispering, and then a noise like someone emptying a bucket of potatoes on the floor. A few more whispers, scuffling sounds, then the crash of a chair overturning and a light appeared under the door, a key turned. Drogo flushed as usual emerged. "Thank God you came." I got him dead centre with a fire extinguisher and went on spraying until I ran out of foam. He stood there, wiping his face and grinning. ''Well, that certainly put the fire out.'''

Separately, Toto finally tracked down Max, to another bedroom and, there being no fire extinguisher available, a bucket of water had to suffice.

When they returned to London, Beaverbrook began making overtures to his son. They were ignored. Then came a handwritten letter, which shows a different side to his character. Full of crossings out, and the second thoughts of a troubled mind, it reads in part:

> *'Stornoway House*
>
> *My Dear Son, if there is any thing [sic] I can do to make your life easier or your vision clearer, let me help you now. Your wish that I should not write or telephone you was observed by me during your stay in Switzerland. Now that you have returned to town, surely you will talk with me again. Apart from your own desires, I would urge you to consider my anxieties - the desperate uncertainties and the exhausting mysteries of your rejection of every avenue of communication. I hope you will come to me. Robertson[19] carries this letter to your flat. He has failed completely to reach you by telephone. Even if*

---

[19] E J Robertson who ran the Daily Express management.

you refuse to see him, I hope you will still come to me.'

Max realised it might be in his best interests to respond, to which his father said, 'Come and see me, my boy.' Max did, and polite conversation followed. To his surprise, Beaverbrook asked how Toto was (very well, thank you), if she had been travelling to the opera (not yet, but soon), and were they still planning to marry (yes). Then Beaverbrook played his ace: 'If you agree not to marry her, I will give you a great deal of money. There will be no other restrictions placed upon you. And I will give her an income for life…' – the equivalent in today's money of £140,000 a year.

Max's plan to lay low had worked, but he wanted to discuss his father's 'offer' with Toto. Years later she explained to Max's granddaughter Laura: *'I loved Max like no other before or after and I would have married him despite what I said. But this was the obvious solution. I didn't want Max to be estranged from his father, so I told him to agree to the offer and I would sign the contract for my part of the deal. I told him that it wouldn't stop us being together. And it didn't.'*

Had Max been playing a high-wire game with his father all along? Or did he run off with Toto as payback for his father being a distant, indifferent parent? It seems it was a genuine case of love dictating the course of events on this occasion – something his father finally faced up to. Just days before his death in 1964, Beaverbrook was asked by The Times: 'What are you most proud of in your life?' The answer: 'Well, I'm most proud of my son, he's a fine fellow. He's a far nicer man than I ever was. A much, much nicer man.'

Now that father and son were on speaking terms again and, with substantially more money in the bank, the couple moved from Oakley Street to a fine apartment in Portman Square, one of London's most prestigious garden squares. Their unmarried status was frowned upon by neighbours, as was the fact that Toto was of mixed race – extraordinary, considering the behaviour, sexual or otherwise, of their class at the time! – but that did not worry them one jot, and they were happy…and happy to allow each other the occasional fling.

In the spring of 1936 Toto went aback to Paris, briefly and alone, where she met a fellow Javanese woman, Hui-Lan Wellington-Koo, 23 years her senior. Hui-Lan, described by the British painter Francis Rose as 'the most beautiful woman in the world', was married to the Chinese ambassador to Paris who had, for 10 months between 1926-27, been president of the Chinese Republic. (As a little girl in Java, Toto had met Hui-Lan's father and remembered him with affection.) The French capital was in great upheaval, with the Communists on the rise as part of the governing Left-wing coalition. Nevertheless, Hui-Lin was still driven around in her white Rolls-Royce by a Dunhill-suited chauffeur, and Toto was a guest at some of the grandest dinner parties of the day, and met the US ambassador to Paris, William Bullitt, one of President Roosevelt's closest friends and confidants, spending a weekend at the chateau in

Chantilly which Bullitt leased. The talk there was of the rise of the Left in France, and of the march of Nazism in Germany…and the threat that it posed to Europe. Toto reported back to Max, who in turn informed his father, and in turn his friends in government.

That summer, Beaverbrook took a party to the Berlin Olympics, an entourage which included Max and his sister Janet but not Toto. That neither surprised nor disappointed her, but she went anyway, as a photographer, and her work appeared in most of the current society magazines. Beaverbrook had been befriended by Germany's new ambassador to Britain, Joachim von Ribbentrop, an urbane Prussian with an excellent command of English.

The two men got on well and had Canada in common: Ribbentrop, who had issued the invitation on behalf of his leader, had worked in Montreal for a bank, and then imported German wines into the country. World War I put paid to that and he retreated to Germany, joining the army on the Eastern Front. Taking up his position as ambassador in London in 1936, he made it his mission to enlist the world's most powerful media mogul to the cause of the Nazis. He was too late. Earlier in the '30s, Beaverbrook had thought that Hitler might be the strong leader Germany needed, but was soon disabused of that view by the violence unleashed on the Jews almost from the moment he became chancellor in 1933. The Express's rival across the street, The Daily Mail, was not so lucky with its proprietor. Lord Rothermere was slavish in his admiration of Mussolini and Hitler and, right up until war was declared, he wrote and ran articles in his newspapers praising Fascism under headlines like 'Hurrah for the Blackshirts'. It was a shameful period for the newspaper of so-called Middle England, and had Rothermere not died in 1940, far away from the action in Bermuda, he might well have faced prosecution after the end of the war.

Therefore, Beaverbrook's acceptance of Hitler's invitation to the Olympics was based on curiosity. As Janet Kidd reported: 'As our party was driven across Berlin to our hotel, father had become increasingly quiet as he noted the swaggering mobs of young men with swastika armbands. Brownshirts were everywhere; I saw notices informing Jews that they entered shops at their own risk.'

Hitler had put much store in the Games; they would show the world what a great power Germany had become under his leadership. He was far from successful, as we know, as witnessed by his humiliation when Jesse Owens, first of the black American superstar athletes, won four gold medals. Less well known is the result of the first and only motoring event at the Olympics. Hitler had ordered that a car rally ending in Berlin be part of the programme, in the full expectation that it would be won by either a Mercedes or an Auto-Union and prove the dominance of Germany's dominant motor industry. In the event, a British Singer Le Mans, a 1.5-litre sports car was victorious. This was a relatively small vehicle, though none the less desirable for that; but it was not a vast engined Mercedes, with its three-pointed star. And worse – *much worse* – it was driven by Betty Haig, grand-niece of World War I field marshal, Lord Haig.

Toto witnessed the reaction of the Nazis to these defeats: increasing censorship, book burnings in the street, and vile anti-Semitic radio broadcasts were stepped up. She also reported back to Max on the proliferation of arms factories, all working 24 hours a day.

Beaverbrook decided he had far better things to do. While Janet went to stay with the Ribbentrops at their vast country estate, staffed by lookalike blond Aryan servants, her father retreated to his hotel, the Adlon. After three days of meetings and phone calls, he was visited by Hermann Goering, who presented him with a tape, suggesting he might like to listen to it… The Nazis had bugged his room for three days.

As for Janet, she was introduced to Hitler by a preening Ribbentrop. 'Hitler got out of his chair (I towered over him),' she recalled, 'and offered his hand. It felt boneless, clammy and soft. There was nothing there, no warmth, no voice, not even an awareness.'

Meanwhile, a close friend of Max's, Bill Hearst, arranged for Max to test some planes for commercial purposes – Lockheeds – in California, so he and Toto set off for San Simeon to stay at Bill's father's legendary estate, Hearst Castle, in 1938. Bill's father Randolph Hearst, like Beaverbrook, had become wealthy beyond even the most extravagant dreams with his publishing empire. He didn't have the Beaver's political clout, but would soon be immortalised by Orson Welles as Citizen Kane – whilst, as we know, Beaverbrook had been granted the dubious honour of being the model for Evelyn Waugh's Lord Copper in Scoop! The castle – Kane's 'Xanadu' in the film – was a ridiculous indulgence with its 50 bedrooms and endless guests, many from Hollywood, who were expected to sit down to a formal dinner every evening. During their visit Toto was asked if she might think about getting back into films, and the answer was an immediate no! But the possibility that she might yet be lured back, despite the firm no, did not enamour her to Marion Davies, Randolph Hearst's mistress, who had been bashing on Hollywood's doors for an age.

Max got stuck into testing some Lockheed planes, comparing them with rival models…much like he did with women. He particularly liked the firm's newest model, a twin-engined Electra – a hugely popular plane at the time – and set a record time for the US west to east coast flight.

Despite the enormous wealth of the Hearst family, it is clear that Bill was very cautious with his own money. On one occasion, writing to Max after he and Toto were back in London, he said: *'Your wires made us wish to hell we could join you, but things have been very busy here this year and I don't believe we will be able to get away at all. We had planned to come over but the steamship lines did not react favourably to our suggestion that they transport us free so we had to change our plans.*

'My best to Toto and yourself, Bill'

After two months in California, with its fabulously reliable fine weather, Max and Toto returned to London. (Beaverbrook wanted his son home and had applied pressure on Randolph Hearst to make that happen.) When they met, Beaverbrook was bearing an offer: return to the fold, managing The Sunday Express. What would Max do? His passion was flying, and he and Toto had adored California…

He accepted, and received this letter the following day from James Whitehouse:

> 'Dear Mr Aitken,
> Please confirm your engagement with SX for £40 a week[20] (three months' notice either side). Starting Sept 1 1938.'

Despite Max's restored responsibilities in the Beaverbrook group, he still had time to live the London social life, with or without Toto, who had thrown herself into helping Jews who had fled Germany for London. Inevitably, he engaged in the occasional fling as this sad letter reveals, sent from the Lausanne Palace Hotel:

> 'Max,
> Of course I got your cable but I could not answer even if I wanted to. Just because you have meant a little bit too much for me and I tried to forget

---

[20] About £160,000 a year today.

you, I can't forget. When last I saw you in London you said you would come to Zurich, possibly you were drunk, because you did not follow me and I have not heard a single word from you, with the result that I was three months ago again in London but I did not ring you up.

Maybe you were mistaken in me, but I really have a heart and a soul.

Just Maud.'

Regardless of his deep love for Toto, it is clear Max found it difficult to entirely abandon his role as handsome lothario and left a few broken hearts in his wake. But in fact the only real and lasting competition Toto had was planes, not other women, and with war looking ever more likely, Max's duties in the Royal Auxiliary Air Force took up many weekends. A letter to his friend Bill Clyde, who later flew with Max in 601 Squadron, is typical of the time:

'Nov 5 1938
In August my father asked me to go back to the SX, which was big news and of course I accepted.

Finally on the Monday Sept 26, now called Black Monday, I went to see Philip at six and he told me that GB had told France to fight and that we would give her our full support. I then went on to Stornoway House and saw my father who was despondent and had practically given up hope for peace. He was pulling out revolvers and talking of turning Cherkley into an armed house etc.

I went on to the Marlborough Club with Mouse and got blind. I could not see anything in the world that could stop war. Mouse[21] and I then went back to my flat and listened to Hitler's speech which Toto translated and the speech was as belligerent and fiery as could be. After such bellicose, Mouse and I had another whisky and soda until in the flat we were all making speeches and shouting "To hell with Hitler!" I then went to Stornoway that night at 12. The whole of Hyde Park was a mass of floodlights, hundreds and hundreds of tipsy men and women digging trenches – everyone was going to knock hell out of the Germans and I think if a vote had been taken on Monday night as to whether the country should go to war or not it would have been 80 per cent in favour.

Following day: Johnny Peel, who is now adjutant, had a terrible time finding the rest of the squadron; no one was in and he did not know what to do so he finally rang the Bag O Nails where there were 16 pilots. He gave the word and the whole Club emptied like in an American movie. People were scrambling for the door except Michael Peacock who remained sound asleep on top of a table in the middle of the floor. Millie had been dishing out free champagne to all the boys. We arrived at Hendon

---

[21] Edward Fielden, later Sir Edward.

all either tipsy or with terrible hangovers. It was very cold and no-one liked the idea of war at all.

All our machines were camouflaged – no numbers and circles painted out – we spent the whole day completing the camouflage, sighting our guns and clipping bullets into the magazines.

We were not allowed to leave the station so with one accord the squadron said "if we cannot go to the women they will come to us." So we decided to give a cocktail party. At this hundreds of women turned up in taxis and every form of vehicle, and the whole squadron became very warlike again immediately. No one doubted there was going to be a war and the people who had done the most flying were most confident.

We were not allowed out of the station and had to be up in the hangar by 8 o'clock Wednesday morning. Then we moved up to Biggin Hill, our war station, but nothing came through and we spent our day firing our guns and being given lectures on German aircraft etc.

On Wednesday evening we had another cocktail party and then came the news that Chamberlain was going to meet Hitler and the Four Power Conference was to take place. The whole squadron was so worked up to war that I think the news was really rather regretted, not in the long run of course, but just for the moment.

We were then disembodied and returned home having had a tremendous 10 days and about £25 better off.'

By the following year Max was away so much, both from Toto and his duties at The Sunday Express, that she resumed her travelling. She wrote this undated letter from the American Hotel in Amsterdam:

> *'Darling,*
>
> *I am sorry you didn't ring last night but you were probably dead tired. Believe it or not but Daddy never arrived. I nearly missed my plane, just caught it by a wisker [sic] as Gill got pinched for speeding as you know. I just sat on the plane when somebody came running on with a telegram. I thought it was from you saying goodbye so opened it only after we got off the ground. It said Daddy had not arrived. My sister-in-law send [sic] it in the hope to stop me coming. Was I mad. She told me everybody of KLM[22]. Now going to stay with all sorts of country bumkins [sic] here. Please send me a wire if you've arrived in Greece.*
>
> *Five years of you and I still miss you. It is a rather nice thought.*
>
> *Be very careful,*
>
> *Love you.'*

Toto's reference to 'five years' is interesting, as all other references make it four years. Maybe her arithmetic was flawed; or had they been lovers for longer than we

---

[22] Where Toto's father was senior director.

understand, running in tandem with her affair with Beaverbrook a few months earlier…?

Back in Paris, Toto stayed with Coco Chanel for three days in her suite at the Ritz. She was well aware of how anti-Semitic Chanel was – sealed by the dodgy deal she had signed with the Jewish Werteimers – but Toto now saw her as a possible avenue to some highly useful information. Chanel was an ardent admirer of Hitler, and was currently the Baron Hans Gunther von Dincklage's lover, Nazi, diplomat and head of the Abwehr in France. In the event, all Toto learned was that her one-time friend was by then even more of a Hitler supporter than she had imagined

Toto then discovered that another couple of Chanel's friends had stayed in the suite next door: Wallis Simpson and her husband the Duke of Windsor had booked in after returning from meeting Hitler at Berchtesgaden. (Winston Churchill and his son Randolph had had dinner there too, with Chanel and Jean Cocteau, the elder Churchill getting drunk and emotional over the fate of the Duke.) Toto listened closely – as she had been advised to by Stewart Menzies – to Chanel enthusing about Hitler, the new Germany, and how the Nazis would reshape Europe. She knew she must keep lines of communication firmly open with her old friend.

CHAPTER 9

THE APPRENTICE SPY

'I was taught not to ask too many questions, just listen.'

– Toto

To observers, Toto may have appeared as little more than a beautiful, wealthy woman sashaying through the ballet and opera houses of Europe. In fact, it was the perfect camouflage.

She enjoyed her evenings in Milan, Venice, Versailles and Berlin, of course, but her real purpose was to mingle – and, if called for, do rather more than mingle – using her exquisite charm and beauty to glean information. And she was hardly coy when it came to lust, so why not use sex for a cause she was convinced was the right one: the fight against fascism in all of its grotesque forms. She may have originally been tasked by her lover, who was still in the throes of a protracted tantrum about her love for his son, but she was hardly going to give up for that reason. Besides, she had Max's encouragement and backing.

The porticoed Berlin State Opera on the Unter den Linden was grand, even by Berlin's imposing standards, its vast, lustrous chandelier shimmering from the central dome above the plush velvet seats. Almost 200 years old, recent performers included Richard Strauss, who was much admired by Hitler…though it was a one-way appreciation. Once at the centre of the city's multi-cultural elite, it was no longer patronised by Jews. Many had fled, and the orchestra and all other performers were Aryan. Dinner jackets were outnumbered by the Nazi dress uniforms worn by the officers – made and marketed by one of their faithful, Hugo Boss – and not all of them were there for the music. Toto's remit was a simple enough operation: to fraternise with these men; and the higher their rank, the better, as the more significant the intelligence should be. Her first breakthrough was not long in coming when she met a young officer, Franz Honnegar of the Abwehr, the German intelligence service, equivalent of the British SIS.

At 26, Honnegar was nearly two years younger than Toto, with fair hair cut short and a long face with fine features, almost identical to those of his countrymen with their permanently raised right arms. Like many before him, he was instantly attracted to her, and two nights later they dined together at the venerable Lutter and Wegner on the Gendarmenmarkt. Its heavy Bavarian food was not to Toto's taste, but that was hardly the point. She casually dropped von Ribbentrop's name into their banter, and told Honnegar that she had met Hitler with

Beaverbrook – she hadn't, but Beaverbrook had, and she knew enough to talk authoritatively on the subject – and that she was worried he was soon to plunge Germany – and Europe – into war. She had a sympathetic audience. Franz Honnegar had spent a year in Sussex, tutoring the young sons of a British diplomat. He had been recruited by the Abwehr on his return, largely for his fluent English and French. He too shared Toto's fears, as did many of his fellow Intelligence officers.

The Abwehr was started in 1920, despite the Treaty of Versailles outlawing Germany from establishing an intelligence agency. Its original purpose was as a defence against foreign espionage, but it soon evolved into a fully operational spy service, particularly wary of the growing Soviet empire. Then, in 1935, Admiral Wilhelm Canaris took charge, and though the Fuhrer did not realise it, he had appointed a clever and highly skilled enemy. Young Honnegar was very much on the admiral's side, though took great care, as Canaris[23] did, to appear loyal to Hitler, seeming to carry out his every order.

As a Dutch passport holder, travel was easy, unlike other nationalities (especially the Poles), so Toto stayed in Berlin for a week, before moving on to Milan and La Scala. She and Franz, not surprisingly, had become lovers,

---

[23] Canaris later saved many Jews from going to their deaths in his master's concentration camps, some of them escaping to England and joining the army to fight against Germany. He was executed for treason in 1944 for, allegedly, his part in the von Stauffenberg plot to assassinate Hitler.

and he had told her that his bosses were not necessarily the Hitler loyalists that the rest of his forces appeared to be; in particular, the cult of the leader was an anathema to the clever old-school admiral. This intelligence was passed back to Max, and onward to Menzies at SIS, and it confirmed what they had already been told. There would be much more to come.

Toto had also cultivated a friendship with one of fascist Italy's most powerful politicians, Count Gian Ciano, son-in-law of Mussolini and, when she met him in 1934, Italian consul to Shanghai. He was back in Rome, briefly, and they sat next to each other at a dinner party hosted by mutual friends. He had married Edda Mussolini four years earlier, but that had not stopped his stream of love affairs, and he was keen that the glorious woman on his right that night would be added to his list. But it was not to be, and soon Toto was an avowed and active enemy of Mussolini and his son-in-law, by then the minister for propaganda and talked of as Il Duce's successor.

It was not just Toto's sensuality, linguistic abilities and ease in Europe's most fashionable drawing rooms that were to her great advantage. Being half Dutch, and Holland being home to many Nazi sympathisers – the National Socialist Movement, the NSB, had been founded in Utrecht in 1931, modelling itself on the Nazis and Mussolini's Fascists – was hugely in her favour. The NSB was not unlike Oswald Mosely's ridiculous Blackshirts in Britain, with Mosely brilliantly parodied as the odious 'Spode' by PG Wodehouse – except that the NSB did have some parliamentary success. Therefore, it was assumed by all that the exquisite Toto was 'one of us', the result of which being that she never needed to ask too many questions; indeed, the flow of information just came naturally, in conversation. It was the perfect setup for an apprentice spy.

Usefully, Toto had secured an interesting tutor in the art of espionage: Moura Budberg, who had first informed Beaverbrook that his son had been seen with her. Moura was part of the Beaver's extensive circle, and she and Toto had become friends. She was one of very few women on earth who could match Toto for attractiveness, mystery and fascination. She was a Ukrainian aristocrat, born in 1891, who by the age of 26 was working at the Russian Embassy in Berlin, where she met Robert Bruce Lockhart, a young British diplomat who was later to work for Beaverbrook on the Evening Standard's gossip column. The couple embarked on an affair, during which time Bruce Lockhart had a rather more serious job: plotting to assassinate Lenin, leader of the nascent Soviet regime. For his troubles he was imprisoned in the Kremlin, and Moura, suspected of being a British agent against the Soviets, was sent to the infamous Lubyanka jail in Moscow. She eventually won her freedom by agreeing to be a double agent, and her lover was exchanged for a Russian spy. Budberg took the truth of her activities to the grave, but what is known is that she was, by 1920, the common-law wife of the writer Maxim Gorky, one of whose great friends was HG Wells.

And here, all roads lead back to Beaverbrook: Wells was a long-standing friend, frequent Cherkley visitor, contributor to the Evening Standard and favourite of the Beaverbrook children. Janet, in particular, remembers him telling them stories in his gentle voice of 'life in other worlds, the stars and the planets where people walked in peace, men and women were equal, and children could rule the universe.' Not exactly *War of the Worlds*…

Gorky had invited Wells to Moscow, where Moura acted as his interpreter and, before long, his lover. When she finally emigrated to Britain in 1933, she and Wells were inseparable, though she did refuse to marry him, and Toto gained a friend, ally and mentor. Interestingly, despite her betrayal, there was no animosity between the two women, maybe because of Budberg's skill with deception. It ensured then, and until she died in 1974, that nobody quite knew the truth about her. Had she been a Soviet double agent all along, despite her tsarist credentials? The art of illusion… It was a lesson which Toto learned, and learned well, in her dealings with the Nazis and Italian Fascists.

Yet Toto had another significant teacher in the art of espionage: Sefton Delmer, the German-born Express foreign affairs doyen. He knew Berlin better than most lifelong residents and, more importantly, what she should be listening and watching for. She recalled: *'Mr Delmer told me not really to ask questions, just to steer any conversation and let it run its natural course. What he meant was not to be too obviously interested. I suppose it must have worked because little by little I got some good information, which I managed to remember before jotting it down when I reached my hotel. At first, I kept those notes in the safe in my room, but when I realised that if they were discovered I would be in big trouble. From that moment I kept them close to me – in my knickers!'*

Toto brought her notes back to London rather than risking telephone calls, which was very wise given the trademark snooping and wire-tapping of the Gestapo, though it was never revealed whether she concealed them in her underwear for the trip back.

Franz Honnegar, her Abwehr lover, would meet Toto whenever she was in Berlin. It was relationship built on mutual respect, and yielded enough information to make her trips to an increasingly frightening city worthwhile. In truth, however, she did not go simply to find out what the Nazis were planning, she went for the opera, and because she was genuinely fond of Honnegar, though not in love with him. (That was taken care of by her dashing 'blade', Max.) It was whilst in Frankfurt for the premiere of Carl Orff's *Carmina Burana*, which she hated, that she was privy to a prime snippet of gossip (and it was only gossip at that time): the Duke and Duchess of Windsor were in talks with a group of supporters who could arrange for the couple to visit Hitler.

She also learned that a Swedish millionaire, Axel Wenner-Gren, a friend of Hermann Goring, was in talks with Colonel Oscar Solbert, acting for the Germans, and a French businessman Charles Bedaux, one of the duke's trusted circle. In the event, Bedaux wrote to Solbert on 23rd August that year, 1937, more than two months after Toto first learned of the possible visit, that Windsor was keen to 'devote his time to the betterment of the masses... the surest way to peace.' This intelligence was quickly relayed to Max, to his father, and Prime Minister Neville Chamberlain. It was met with horror in the Cabinet, and by the reluctant new king, George VI. Beaverbrook was not surprised. He had got to know the duke well in his brief reign as Edward VIII, and had played a considerable role in trying to persuade the British public – a great many of whom were his readers – to accept Mrs Simpson as his wife. To this end, he had worked with Rothermere, and they were near to winning the argument when the king decided enough was enough and abdicated.

It was this piece of intelligence which persuaded Beaverbrook that Toto had the makings of a skilled agent, and immediately put the staff of the Express office in Berlin at her disposal. Toto's information proved totally accurate, as on 11th October that year the Windsors arrived in Berlin for 12 days, culminating with a meeting with Hitler at Berchtesgaden, his Bavarian retreat. It was later said that Hitler had promised the duke a return to the throne should Germany win any future conflict. The Windsors spent time with as odious a cast of characters as could be assembled: Goebbels, Speer and Goering. A visit to the Hitler youth academy was also arranged, and the duke gave the Nazi salute wherever he went. The trip prompted great sadness on the part of Churchill, and Beaverbrook too, who also liked the duke very much.

Toto told Max she had slept with Honnegar, and added that she would not hesitate to go to bed with others if it helped in her new role as a spy. She knew he was enjoying himself in London, anyway. Fidelity was not high on either of their lists. But genuine love and affection very much was.

CHAPTER 10

THE DRUMS OF WAR

'Despite being in the Gestapo, he seemed decent and was very kind to me…'

— Toto

By the beginning of 1939 few people had any real doubt that war in Europe was inevitable. The continent was a cauldron of hate and violence. In Germany, Adolf Hitler, since becoming chancellor six years earlier, had abolished democracy, and was brutally ruling a country that made outcasts of many of its citizens; or, according to him, 'non-citizens'. Under the 1935 Nuremberg Laws, Jews and gypsies were instantly targeted for persecution. Three years later Austria was annexed, with Czechoslovakia his next target. Italy had an odious Fascist dictator, Benito Mussolini, who had used poisonous gas while invading and then occupying a powerless Ethiopia in 1935; in Spain Franco was winning the civil war that had been raging for three years, aided by Hitler and Mussolini. Britain and France had, in effect, been standing idly by.

When Britain, France, Italy and Germany had signed the Munich Agreement in September 1938 – almost immediately known as the Munich Betrayal – and Prime Minister Neville Chamberlain returned to London brandishing his piece of paper stating 'there will be no war', it was immediately apparent that it was not worth the paper it was written on. But some people, who should have known better, believed it. Foremost was Beaverbrook, who oversaw coverage of the 'settlement' in the Daily Express under the headline 'There Will Be No European War This Year or Next Year Either'.[24] He was right about one thing: there was no war in 1938, but mistaken in every other regard.

But it was not just Europe in turmoil. Russia was under the rule of the most authoritarian regime yet seen in history, with millions of people sent to the labour camps, meeting their fate on the whim of Stalin. Few would return. Russia's neighbour China was at war with imperialist Japan. The world was an uncertain place, and Toto now felt it too, on a deeply personal level. Her travels across Europe as the seductive spy had given Max time for reflection. Much as he loved her and she loved him, they could not marry unless they were prepared to defy Beaverbrook and lose their financial lifelines. Max knew marriage had never really been on Toto's to-do list, nor did she want children. He, on the other hand, thought he should find a suitable bride and in 1939,

---

[24] The headline still tops the 'How Wrong Can You Be' charts.

while Toto was in Holland, he married the (inevitably) beautiful debutante, Cynthia Monteith. The Toto-Max love affair was over.

When Britain finally declared war on Germany on 3rd September 1939, as a result of Hitler's invasion of Poland, Toto was in Amsterdam visiting her father. It would be the last time she saw him as two years later he died, at the age of 62, eight years after her mother Catharina.

She had been in Holland to meet Ernst Hofmeyer, a Gestapo officer stationed there to liaise with the Dutch sympathisers. Blissfully unaware of the fact, Hofmeyer was the source of a steady stream of new information being sent to London, direct to Beaverbrook, wired by an Express reporter stationed in the city. Later that year the couple would go to Paris, where Hofmeyer met von Dincklage. But at his side was Coco Chanel, and little did Chanel know, but Toto was in contact with Hofmeyer for the very same reason she was. Toto knew precisely why Coco had teamed up with Dincklage: to protect herself and all her interests. The two women were on opposite sides of the seething world, and only Toto was privy to the secret.

Hofmeyer and Toto saw each other occasionally, with some useful, though not startling, information resulting. It was a brief affair, lasting just three months, which ended when Toto travelled to Italy.

Within a year Hofmeyer was sent to the Eastern Front when Russia joined the Allies in 1941 and was killed in early 1942. As Toto told Laura: *'Despite being in the Gestapo, he seemed decent and was very kind to me. He was sophisticated and we had much in common, so much so I introduced him to my father. He helped me with the paperwork I needed to travel through Europe and I have no doubt that he would have tried to protect me if he could. But with his death I lost my protector. How different things might have been.'*

In June 1940, Mussolini joined Hitler in the war, just as Toto was visiting wealthy Hungarian art collector friends in Florence. Max was now married, and in the air with 601 Squadron, the so-called Millionaires' Squadron made up of many (highly skilled) aristocrats, was on his way to being a genuine RAF war hero. His experience as a pilot, beginning at Cambridge with the Auxiliary Air Squadron and enhanced by his time with Lockheed in California, made him formidable.

The Beaver, smarting from the embarrassment of the Munich headline, was about to play his very considerable part in the Allies' eventual victory as Minister for Aircraft Production under his closest friend Winston Churchill, who had replaced Chamberlain as prime minister.

And Coco Chanel? Immensely rich, and ensconced in the luxury of the Ritz, by then the headquarters of senior Nazis in newly-occupied France.

Historical notes on the Ritz describe, without a hint of irony, the rate paid by the Nazis for their accommodation as 'favourable'.

Toto's arrival in Italy's historic and most beautiful city, at just 32 years old, triggered a dramatic chain of events that would change her life forever. She knew the risks she was taking. She was bisexual, and bi-racial, and that was certainly not the Aryan ideal of the Nazis or their slavish followers under Mussolini. She was also aware of the internment camps in Germany and Poland, though few knew yet what horrors were concealed within their walls and fences.

Despite a gilded childhood, she had encountered the cruel and ignorant jibes of being 'mixed-race' by those stupid enough to taunt her, and she had learned to use her three outstanding qualities to field the ignorance of her ridiculers: beauty, brains and bravery. It had taken bravery to defy her parents and move to Paris in 1928, unchaperoned and just 19; and, in particular, to go against their advice and seek work as a model, seen by many as no better a 'profession' than a prostitute. But not only did she succeed, she succeeded spectacularly. In fact, she conquered royally in the French capital, entrancing both men and women to sit atop the city's beautiful and cultural elite.

No doubt, Toto was a woman who knew her own mind and was not to be diverted from following it. She was prepared to take risks, but calculated ones that meant she avoided scandal – in the shape of the notorious Tallulah Bankhead, for instance – and she did not really care for the vacuous opinions of others. And she never stopped learning, never more so than during her 10 months at the side of Beaverbrook. Her time with him was like a mighty crash course in politics and current affairs, sitting at tables with Winston Churchill and Stewart Menzies of MI6 on the one side, and Count Dino Grandi, von Ribbentrop and Mussolini on the other. Most importantly: she was never, ever in doubt which side she was on.

When she slept with the enemy she did so as a spy and not as a pleasure seeker, though she never denied that the job came with benefits. And if she was regarded by some as 'a good-time girl' she knew better: as far as she was concerned she was simply 'a good person'. Why else had she agreed to tour the capitals of Europe in the late 1930s risking her life as she searched for pointers to the war that would inevitably follow?

Hitler had visited Florence in 1938, to be greeted by cheering Fascists flying both the Italian and Nazi flags. Only the brave Archbishop of Florence, Elia Della Costa, stood firm. By any standards, he was a remarkable man: during World War I he helped look after wounded soldiers and tended orphaned children; throughout the Mussolini years, Della Costa was vehemently anti-Fascist, at great risk to himself; and when Hitler strutted through Florence, he closed the doors and windows of the episcopal palace and all his churches, much to the fury of the government and many in the Catholic hierarchy who supported both Hitler and Mussolini.

For Della Costa, empty gestures were pointless. He was indeed saintly, but he was also practical, and during World War II helped save thousands of Italians from execution at the hands of the Fascists. He encouraged his priests and parishioners to shield Jews, and later set up an elaborate rescue network for them to escape. Many were sheltered within his own palace. But nothing illustrates his bravery (and ingenuity) better than his enlisting of Gino Bartali, winner of the Tour de France, to deliver fake papers for Jews to flee. His logic was that no soldier would dare stop Bartali, a national hero, and he was right. The man would also become one of Toto's great allies.

Toto arrived in Florence, where she was booked into the Grand Hotel Baglioni, surrounded by the stunning treasures of the city. She was ready for whatever or whomever was waiting for her. She detested Italy's particular brand of Fascism. Mussolini had decreed that women 'were not capable of great spiritual ideas or deep thought' and were certainly not allowed to enter politics. From legislation introduced in 1926, 'inferior' women were excluded from various jobs, especially in the professions; they were officially 'biologically lesser' humans, and if they wished to go to university, they would be charged double the fees of men. And, in a sinister parallel to the perversion of today's Islamic extremists, the penal code of 1930 made it legal for a man to kill his wife, daughter or sister to defend his own honour. Women – if they managed to avoid being murdered by a male family member – were assigned the job of making babies, preferably boys, who would grow up to be loyal soldiers fighting for this odious philosophy.

Not satisfied with his treatment of half the population of his country, in 1938 Il Duce emulated Hitler's laws on

Jews by forcing through anti-Semitic legislation, closing schools, universities and many non-menial jobs to the Jewish community. It acted as a recruiting campaign for the liberals in the country to unite and organise against. This beautiful country, once the most civilised and cultured in the world, lush with natural abundance and the finest architecture and art created over two millennia, was now a corrupt basket case led by a madman.

Toto was very aware of how Mussolini dealt with anti-Fascists, especially the women among them: they would be arrested and, if they escaped death, would be shipped off to penal colonies on the many islands in the Mediterranean, tiny dots in the sea such as Asinara and Ponza, which today are among the most beautiful destinations in Europe for holidaymakers. They would be labelled as 'prostitutes', 'unnatural mothers' (whatever that meant), 'hags' and 'steeped in vice'. The dictator's spies were everywhere and being a liberal in Italy in the 1930s was a very dangerous business.

The next decade would see a descent into the darkest recesses of human behaviour, and it was this world that Toto was now living, and spying, in.

Greatest allies: Beaverbrook and Churchill onboard HMS Prince of Wales in 1941 during the Atlantic Conference with President Roosevelt. Churchill relied on his friend both in and out of Cabinet. The Beaver never let him down.

Father and son: The Beaver had been a typical Edwardian father who played little part in raising his children. Later, however, he grew very close to Max and described him as 'a far, far better man than I ever was.'

The vital link: One of the 130 ft-tall masts at Beaverbrook's radio shack at Cherkley, his country estate. Three masts monitored radio traffic during the war. It was Toto's only link with London and the War Cabinet.

Beguiling: Toto at the height of her modelling career in Paris, 1934. She was just 26 and about to meet the man who would change her life for ever: Lord Beaverbrook.

Reluctant star: Toto in a publicity shot for the Korda film *The Private Life of Don Juan*. She hated the process of film making, it bored her, and her role ended up on the cutting room floor.

Agent Westminster: Coco Chanel pictured in 1944 in Paris. By then she knew her war was all but lost. Could she escape the punishment that seemed inevitable?

Friends and enemies: Chanel hunting with the two Churchills, Randolph, left, and Winston in the late 1920s. Did her friendship with her admirer Winston save her when the war was over?

Free at last: Women at Ravensbruck are finally told that they are to be released. Many could never bring themselves to speak of the horrors inflicted on them there.

Dah…ling: Tallulah Bankhead pictured in 1932 before she met Toto. It was Tallulah who introduced her to Beaverbrook and changed the course of Toto's life.

First Night: Tallulah Bankhead, left, and Toto at the premiere of *The Private Life of Don Juan*, London 1934. The private life of Bankhead was far racier than the Don's.

Be very careful: Toto's letter to Max from Amsterdam is undated but it is clearly from 1939.when she was in Holland. Her sign-off 'be very careful' illustrates her concern for him as he prepared for battle in the skies.

to day of K.L.M. went to meet Daddy including the boss Plesman and he wasn't there. It wasn't his fault. as he travels for nothing he had to give his seat. but K.L.M. ought to have known. Now it seems he is coming on Tuesday. Its lovely weather so I am going to stay with all sort of country bumkins friends. leaving this afternoon. I think you better use 44 apolla laan amsterdam adress. as I'll be staying there mostly. Please send me a wire if you've arrived in france. Thursday next is my girls friends birthday promised to stay for that. as I don't think you'll be back before that. Darling 5 years of you and I still miss you it is rather nice though. be very carefull. love you monks

STORNOWAY HOUSE,
CLEVELAND ROW,
ST JAMES'S.

My dear Son

If there is anything
I can do to make your
life easier or your vision
clearer, let me help you. *now*

I have observed your
wish to withdraw from
conversation with me and
~~It is true that you~~

You wish that I should
not write or telephone you

A troubled mind: Beaverbrook's letter to Max pleading with him
to meet. The second thoughts and crossings out show just how
unhappy he was over the breakdown of their relationship.

Observed

was ~~cannot~~ sent by me
during your stay in
Switzerland.

But Now that you have
returned to town, surely
you will talk with me
again.

Apart from your own
desires I would urge you
to consider my anxieties
& the desperate uncertainty
~~uncertainta~~ & the ~~expanding~~
expanding mysteries of your
~~silent rejection~~ rejection of
every avenue of communication

STORNOWAY HOUSE,
CLEVELAND ROW,
St JAMES.S.

Robertson carries this
letter to you past, after
~~his~~ He has failed
completely to reach you
by telephone.

Even If you ~~refuse to~~ see
him I ~~hope you will come to me.~~
~~assist in my efforts~~
~~unless I know that~~
~~by you have been~~
~~experienced~~

PART TWO
IT WAS THE WORST OF TIMES

CHAPTER 11

THE RITZ OR THE MOUNTAIN LAIR

*'Once I was in [...] it could never have been a case
of dipping in and dipping out.'*

– Toto

Toto met Elizabeth Eichmann in Florence, a young
German woman who had managed to get permission
to leave the country with her sister Ingerborg to study
in Italy. The three women became great friends and
Elizabeth accompanied Toto to a meeting of Blackshirts
posing as Fascist sympathisers – easily done, as Toto
spoke perfect Italian and Elizabeth was seen as a 'good
German'. The information they gleaned was relayed to
London through a ramshackle messenger system devised
by the young leader of a local resistance group, Lorenzo
Rado. The group was a mix of local boys, several
Communists among them, who had no desire to join
Mussolini's army, and deserters. They were organised
and sustained by women who foraged for food; anything
which would provide protein, including snails, frogs,

hedgehogs, squirrels, and even the occasional guinea pig. There were mushrooms and chestnuts, too, and the occasional cup of goat's milk and local wine, as well as rice and maize, so polenta was a constant. In the smart restaurants of Europe, many of these ingredients would end up on expensive and fashionably artisan menus. In 1940 they were staple items.

Elizabeth Eichmann remembered: 'I adored Toto, she was so special and determined, unique in every way. I was much more reserved and shy. She had a way of seeing the light in the midst of a storm. Her combination of strength and humour was reassuring during this very stressful time. We were soulmates from the moment we met. I was amazed by Toto's courage, she exhibited remarkable sangfroid and risked everything to stand up for her convictions.'

Three weeks after that first meeting, listening to the Blackshirts, Toto made a momentous decision: she left the Baglioni hotel and joined the Resistance. She recalls: *I thought I could join for a while and then report back from the hotel. I simply hadn't thought it through properly because that sort of arrangement was simply not possible. For a start, once I was in I became totally immersed and it could never have been a case of dipping in and dipping out. And leaving these brave people would have been a betrayal of both them and my own conscience. So once I was in I was in for good. Or at least until events took over.'

Toto, used to the finest foods and the fabulous luxury of the best hotels was now dining on roasted hedgehog and sleeping wherever it was deemed safe enough to lay her head.

Tuscany, particularly the area between Florence and Prato, had a history of radicalism and resistance. When the Fascists first came to power in the 1920s, there were numerous scuffles and several deadly gun battles; in fact, and shortly before Toto arrived, 12 partisans had been ambushed by Fascists. Two were killed, and three wounded and taken to prison. This was no game, and certainly not for a girl from Miss Crozier's Academy for Young Ladies. But Toto had never been content with the norm, so it was no surprise – at least to herself – that she threw her lot in with the Resistance.

The seeds had been sown in 1938, when she and Max had attended a banquet at London's Savoy Hotel. Thanks to the slip of a clumsy waiter who spilled a drop of sauce on her silk shoulder wrap, she briefly met the very apologetic head waiter of banqueting, a small, modest man called Fortunato Picchi. When the dinner had ended, Picchi came over to express his apologies again and the pair spoke briefly. He was 12 years her senior, from Carmignano in Tuscany, and had been wounded and awarded for his gallantry fighting for the Allies in World War I. She learned in those few short minutes that he was a committed and, by now, absolute Anglophile who had left Italy for London in 1921 to work in the capital's great hotels, including the Hyde Park, the Ritz and the Savoy.

When she asked him why he was not in Italy, Picchi, also an amateur sculptor, revealed his deep-rooted hatred of Fascism. The conversation ended as quickly as it had begun, but it had a profound effect on Toto, so much so that she told Laura Aitken she'd decided she must return to help with the fight against Mussolini: *'What Mr Picchi told me left a mark. I can't be sure why it was so striking, maybe because he was nobody's idea of a hero. Small and balding, but his decency radiated from him. I have never forgotten him.'*

When Italy entered the war allied with Germany, Picchi's views on Fascism did not prevent him from being rounded up by the UK authorities and sent to an internment camp on the Isle of Man as an enemy alien. After six months, however, he was sent back to London, the authorities secure in the knowledge that, far from posing any threat, he could be a great asset for the Allies – and sent him to train for the Intelligence Corps. He impressed those watching him, and it was said: 'An idealist, in many ways more English than the English […] he cannot allow failure […] is prepared to share in all of England's trials […] has excellent English.' From there Picchi was sent to train as a parachutist and joined X Troop, 11th Special Air Service, much to his delight.

Picchi was selected for Operation Colossus, intended to destroy a 100-metre stretch of aqueduct in Southern Italy, vital for feeding water to the Italian naval bases at Brindisi, Taranto and Bari. Alas, the operation failed, and on 14th February 1941 Italy announced the capture of a party of British parachutists. They walked for days across mountains in the hope of reaching safety, but were caught and driven to Calitri, then on to Naples for interrogation. Picchi failed to pass himself off as French to his accusers, and was taken from the Regina Coeli prison into the countryside where, on a cold morning at dawn on 6th April, he was tied to a chair and shot in the back. His mother later received this letter from him:

> *'My dearest Mamma,*
>
> *After so many years you receive from me a letter.*
>
> *I'm sorry dear Mamma for you and for all at home for this disaster and the pain it will bring. By now it is over for me, all that remains is the world of pain or pleasure. I do not care much about dying. I repent my actions because I have always loved my country and must now be recognised as a traitor. Yet in all conscience I do not think that is so.*
>
> *Forgive me dear Mamma and remember me to all. I ask you especially for your forgiveness and your blessing which I need so much. Kiss all my brothers and sisters and to you dear Mamma a hug, hoping with the grace of God to be reunited in heaven.*
>
> *Your child, Fortunato.*
>
> *Long live Italy!!'*

As a postscript to this story, when Picchi's landlady in London, Florence Lantieri, found out about his death, she placed this notice in The Times:

'PICCHI. On Palm Sunday 1941, Fortunato Picchi sacrificed his life for the cause of freedom. A brave man of high ideals. Until the day breaks, dear – F'

Toto, like the fearless and determined Picchi, knew there was great danger in fighting wickedness. It had ended in death by firing squad for him, and she was well aware she might meet the same fate. But she didn't let that stop her. It was the biggest decision of her life, and there was no going back.

Her fellow Resistance fighter, Lorenzo Rado, was typical of many partisans in the small villages around Prato and Florence which nestled in the foothills of Monte Morello. Most were poor farm labourers, content with the lowly living conditions because, unlike Toto, they had never known comfort, let alone luxury. They were poorly equipped, too, though army defectors brought rifles and ammunition when they could.

It has been said that to help fund the cause Toto sold her furs and jewellery. But where and to whom she could sell is something of a mystery, given that she was either permanently on the move or in hiding. What is known is that she received funds, either from the government or from Beaverbrook himself, probably dropped with arms and other supplies by British planes. But this must have been spasmodic, if at all, and understandably there is no record of dates.

This small group of Resistance warriors had one advantage: Toto's connections with Max and

Beaverbrook, and therefore the War Cabinet. And the radio messages were two-way, as she was able to tell Cherkley of the Resistance's progress in Tuscany – which in truth amounted to being a 'plain bloody nuisance' as one officer called it. But being a nuisance by blowing up supplies and spreading anti-Mussolini propaganda was useful: it was all part of waging war. Their location could also be broadly tracked, but as the Intelligence services had so far failed to organise a unit of experienced Italian-speaking operators to plant in Italy, they were on their own. It was not for want of trying, however. Churchill was growing impatient that little was happening to help the partisans. There had been an unsuccessful attempt to recruit Italians living in Egypt on the basis that not enough of them were anti-Fascist; similarly, a trawl of the 100,000 Italians in Canada had come to nought. The situation would improve greatly with Special Operations Executive training schools from Devon to the Scottish Highlands, teaching the dark arts of subversion, assassination, bomb making and booby trapping. But that would not happen until the arrival in London in 1942 of the remarkable Emilio Lussu, a Sardinian who finally convinced Hugh Dalton, the Cabinet minister who established the SOE, that setting up operations in Italy was a viable option.

Until that happened, Toto and her raggle-taggle Resistance friends were on their own, relying only on their daring and beliefs. In short, with the fall of France, Belgium, Luxembourg and the Netherlands, and Italy's entry into the war, Britain was alone and relied on the Resistance in those countries, particularly in France and Italy, to do as much damage as possible before it would set foot in continental Europe in 1943. By then the economic and military power of the US and the Soviet Union would have joined the embattled Churchill. Before that, however, the fear among the War Cabinet was that the Communists among the Resistance would eventually steer Italy towards Moscow. But that was not a prime consideration for the partisans, or for Toto. Their priority was to harass the Fascists at every possible turn and save Italian Jews from death.

By the time Toto was a fully-fledged Resistance fighter, Beaverbrook had built a monitoring station, his 'Radio Shack', in the grounds of the Cherkley estate. It was a simple single-storey brick-built hut with three masts, each 130 feet tall, with the latest radio equipment – extremely sophisticated for the time. Three men were employed to monitor all traffic on three shifts over 24 hours, and the transcriptions were passed to one of the Beaver's many secretaries for his scrutiny. Whatever was deemed relevant was then relayed to Churchill or Stewart Menzies, head of SIS. Toto would send her messages back to Britain, with news of the partisans' efforts; but, maybe more importantly, she would receive orders for them from Britain.

Interestingly, the Radio Shack was demolished in 1991, but nearby stands a fine house and adjacent studio owned by the distinguished sculptor Jonathan

Kenworthy. His father Alexander was a Daily Express correspondent, and early authority on the then Common Market, so much so that the Beaver regularly turned to him for his thoughts. In the late 1970s, Jonathan Kenworthy was approached by an elderly Australian named Leslie Pratt, who recounted listening to the wretched blethering of William Joyce, the American-born, Irish-raised, British-educated (and British-executed) Fascist who broadcast messages to the UK from Berlin during the war with the aim of convincing Britain that the game was up. Pratt told Kenworthy: 'I said to Lord Beaverbrook that there's this bloke haw-hawing away. "Then that's what we shall call him, Lord Haw Haw!" was his lordship's response.'

Back in Tuscany, Toto visited Archbishop Della Costa. They discussed their efforts, and the archbishop arranged for Toto to meet Leonardo Mozzi, a former Italian army corporal who had returned to the family farm near Prato in 1937 when his father had died. He had Jewish friends who had been rounded up and deported, probably to their deaths, and he was determined to do all he could to prevent that happening to others. The archbishop was his great ally, and together they had saved, by 1941, at least 30 people, including children. Mozzi was a good-looking young man and undoubtedly intelligent. He was certainly not a 'Max', the epitome of the suave and urbane chaps of his class and era, but there could be no doubting the ex-corporal's decency and good intentions.

Toto was immediately drawn to Mozzi's courage, and motives, and soon after meeting him began her next affair – though the great houses and fine hotels of Europe had been traded for modest farm cottages, and even one of the numerous caves in the Tuscan hills and mountains, temporary hideouts for the fighters.

Leonardo Mozzi was much enamoured by this fabulous woman who had come into his life so suddenly, though he doubted her at first. Was she really a Fascist spy? If she was who she said she was, why on earth had she abandoned the life of comfort, pleasure and money she had enjoyed for more than three sophisticated decades? It did not take long for him to be convinced of her legitimacy, however, and the archbishop urged him to have faith in her. They were together as much as was possible, for five intense, immensely interesting months, and in that time he could not fail to be impressed by Toto's great ability to watch and learn. She had God-given powers of observation, and the capacity to remember what she had seen and heard without putting pen to paper until it was safe to do so. Their radio transmitter was crude compared to Beaverbrook's outfit, and required almost daily 'modifications', but with much coaxing to life they could send reports to the Cherkley monitors.

Their primary task at this early stage of the war was to get as many Italian Jews out as possible, some to Britain, others to relatives in New York. London's support for the Italian Resistance, however, remained confused, and confusing. Churchill believed that Italians should rally round their king, Vittorio Emanuele; but the monarch had lost the trust of many Resistance fighters because it was he who had appointed Mussolini and had singularly failed to curb the dictator's worst Fascist excesses. And the prime minister was anxious, of course, that the Communists, who were so prominent in the movement, would eventually lead Italy to Moscow. Churchill, therefore, concentrated Britain's efforts on aiding the French Resistance, and it was not until after the liberation of Italy in 1943 that the Allies' assistance for the Italians featured more consistently.

In the meantime, Toto and her comrades were very much alone, conducting a lone, courageous operation from the farms and hills and caves above Tuscany.

*

At the Ritz, in occupied Paris, 650 miles away, Coco Chanel was in full rant: her seamstresses had downed scissors in a strike, joining much of the entire French workforce who were demanding better wages, a shorter week and paid holidays. Their action had shocked Chanel; she patronisingly regarded them as 'my girls', and her eventual and inevitable capitulation to their demands had struck her hard, and deeply. But the outbreak of war, with German tanks in the city, gave her the opportunity for revenge: she sacked her entire female workforce, including the cutters, the stitchers and boutique girls.

Chanel was by now 55 years old – though she still had the figure of a woman two decades younger – and was convinced the war would put an end to fashion. It was over, forever, as far as she was concerned. Her frame of mind was not helped by the competition she had faced from Elsa Schiaperrelli, whom she disparagingly dismissed as 'l'Italienne', and whose bold, colourful designs had become a favourite of the rich and beautiful.

She couldn't have been more mistaken, of course, and later she acknowledged her dreadful mistake: 'I was so stupid, such a dummy about life. That will be a lesson to me. Whatever happens hereafter I will go on making clothes. The only thing I believe in.'

Clothes were not quite the only thing she believed in, though… She believed, totally and without reservation, that the war was caused by the Jews and Communists, and that Hitler would soon sort them out, for once and for all. The influences that shaped her despicable view had almost all been violently anti-Semitic: the bullying nuns at her orphanage, the appalling 'Bendor', Duke of Westminster, and her most recent lover, Paul Iribe.

Keeping company at the Ritz alongside Coco were the very rich, including the artist Jean Cocteau and various American industrialists. During Allied air raids, these guests quickly assembled in the basement, taking their champagne or Cognac with them. In painful contrast, most French families ate meat just twice a week, if they were very lucky, and the coffee they drank was mixed with chicory root. Britain was faring no better, with the introduction of food rationing and severely limited fuel. And as for the appalling poverty and starvation across whole swathes of Europe…

Chanel's hardship, apart from the rebellion of her girls, was the call-up of her chauffeur to war, and the decision by her two maids, sisters Germaine and Jeanne, to escape Paris for the relative safety of their home village. Disgruntled, Coco hired a new chauffeur and had her copious luggage packed. Paris was by then a deserted city. All of the shops were closed, including her own boutiques; the cabs were gone, and the telephone lines cut. Even the wandering street dogs were nowhere to be seen. And upon rising one morning, a thick black bank of smoke hung low over the City of Light: civil servants had burned their ministry's papers before the enemy arrived. In fear of the rumoured air raids, and dismayed at the state of her beloved Paris, Coco joined four million of her fellow citizens in the mass exodus from the city and the surrounding countryside. She was driven 500 miles in a Cadillac to Corbere in the Pyrenees where her extended family lived, along with her first lover, Etienne Balsan.

On 17th June 1940 France surrendered, seven weeks after German soldiers first marched into Paris. Five days later, an armistice was formally signed by the new leader, Marshal Philippe Petain, and swastika flags flew from the Eiffel Tower and along the great boulevards. Within 24 hours, Adolf Hitler was driving down the Champs-Élysées in triumph, goose-stepping Wehrmacht troops alongside. The spa town of Vichy was the unlikely new seat of Petain's government which, within three months, would bring in the Statute on Jews, banning them from high profile positions in society, such as the press, legal and medical professions, and the army.

At the luxurious Chateau Palasse in Corbere, Chanel paced and pondered her future. She desperately wanted to return to Paris to supervise her perfume business, the main source of her fortune now that her couture business had been plunged into silence. Consequently, in late July she ordered her chauffeur to find enough petrol to get them to Paris, stopping first at Vichy. She found the place full of prostitutes availing themselves of the newly installed German bureaucrats; or was that the other way around?

When she arrived at the Ritz, she discovered it was guarded by stiff German troopers and flanked with sandbags. 'Guests' were mostly high-ranking German officers, and three hundred thousand German soldiers and officials occupied surrounding buildings and houses, which had been forcibly seized.

Mercedes limousines queued outside. And on the register of 'welcome residents', one name stood out: her own.

Two women, two lives; once in high society tandem, now as diametrically opposed as day from night.

CHAPTER 12

TWO LIVES, TWO PATHS

'Coco really only had two loves...herself and her fashion house.'
— Coco's friend, Lady Iya Abdy

Chanel's suite consisted of rooms 227 and 228, near that of the pro-Nazi Dubonnet drinks family, and Fern Bedoux, American wife of the fabulously rich Frenchman Charles Bedoux, who, after the war, committed suicide when charged with trading with the enemy. Fern Bedoux was a proud German collaborator, and it was she and her husband who hosted the wedding of the Windsors and subsequently helped to organise their visit to Hitler. Almost all the other inhabitants were from the upper echelons of the triumphant Nazis including, when they visited Paris, Joseph Goebbels and Hermann Goring. They dined on *filet de sole au vin de Rhin* — filet of sole in dry Rhine wine; how very patriotic — with peas, asparagus and hollandaise sauce. As one bloated, gloating officer said: 'In times like these, to eat well and eat a lot gives a feeling of power.'

Now reinstalled in her precious Paris, Chanel was in the mood for love. Enter, or rather re-enter, Baron Hans Gunther von Dincklage, back in town from a spectacularly unsuccessful trip to Switzerland. He had travelled there posing as a businessman to report back on Swiss defences. He and his masters in Berlin had underestimated Swiss efficiency, however, and he was arrested, but not for long. The view was taken that the authorities did not want to incur the wrath of Hitler, and the Abwehr agent was swiftly sent back to Paris. The man was a willing shoulder for her to lean on.

Coco had an immediate task for the Abwehr man: organise the release of her French army soldier nephew, Andre Palasse, from a prisoner of war camp in Germany where he been taken after capture on the Maginot Line.[25] Dincklage was, in effect, her conduit to the German High Command in Paris, and his usefulness perfectly illustrates the view of Chanel's friend Lady Iya Abdy, the Russian-born model and actress, who said: 'Coco really had only two loves…herself and her fashion house. Everything else was merely passion, weakness, adventures without a future, and calculated liaisons.' Dincklage fell into the latter category, though Chanel claimed theirs was a 'true love affair'.

The two lovers continued to live a life most Parisians could not: the opera, nightclubs, Maxim's and, of course, heat and light in their hotel rooms and houses, petrol for their chauffeur-driven cars and the finest food. Coco also

---

[25] He succeeded, which tells us a lot about the Chanel relationship with the Nazis.

owned 31 Rue Cambon, a brief step from the Ritz. On the ground floor was her original boutique, and upstairs an exquisite apartment where she entertained friends and high-ranking Nazi officers. She had kept her cook on, and a maid who waited on the table; the music was provided courtesy of Dincklage on the piano. When not 'at home' or in her Ritz suite, the couple would dine at the German Embassy in great splendour, with abundant champagne. It was there that, according to author Ian Ousby, she 'indulged in anti-Semitic diatribes'.

*

For Toto, Paris, London, Milan, Florence and the Baglioni...they were a distant memory. She was living the life she had chosen, but she was unkempt and on edge. Food was scarce, and strange, and she had lost weight – and there wasn't much to lose. In her own words:

> *'I think I missed not visiting the hairdresser most, though one of the village girls occasionally cut it. But we were moving around so much it wasn't really possible. I missed Max of course and prayed that he would be safe. That was my constant thought. I understood why our relationship had to end, he had to try for the conventional life of a wife and children, but my love for him would never dim. Oh, and I missed privacy. There certainly wasn't much of that living from place to place with so many men.*

I was frightened much of the time. My friend Leo[26] had friends who had been arrested by the Fascists and sent to prison before transfer to concentration camps. One of them was someone called Pietro[27], who had fought in the Spanish Civil War and on his return was arrested and sent to a foreign labour camp in France. I think he died in Germany, as so many of his friends did. We all knew what we were risking, but we knew what we were doing was right. It got much, much worse later when the Germans were fighting in Italy. But at least I could sometimes communicate with England so I knew they were fighting hard too and we had not been forgotten.'

In January 1941 her fears were realised: she was arrested when Mussolini's police rounded up eight partisans, six men and two women, including Toto. They were taken to Florence and split up. All were questioned. The men were beaten; the women degraded. After three days Toto was transferred to San Vittore prison on the outskirts of Milan, 120 miles away, in a truck on icy roads in the middle of a particularly harsh winter night. The prison was a forbidding-looking building with its mediaeval-style watchtowers, and Toto was locked in a freezing, filthy cell that bore the foul evidence of the previous occupant. She had grown used to living in austere circumstances in the hills of Florence, but nothing

---

[26] Leonardo Mozzi
[27] Research shows this was possibly Pietro Aureli from Florence.

could have prepared her for a straw mattress and dirty, stinking blankets, a basin and a bucket of icy water, and a lavatory in the corner. The window was broken, and the wind was bitter. Toto ran on the spot and danced the Charleston to try to keep warm, and to raise her spirits.

She was constantly questioned about her activities, and her guards took delight in sexually harassing her. Her friend, Lady Deirdre Curteis, said, 'Toto suffered terrible humiliation at the hands of her jailors. She told me that the Italians there were far from the charming and endearing people of their national reputation.' Amongst the questions about her reasons for being in Italy, her interrogators seemed fixated on Beaverbrook. She later said it was as if they wanted her to return to England to spy on *him* and the British war plans and inform the Fascists.

Two months later Toto was transferred halfway down the length of Italy to Bolsena, near Viterbo in Lazio. Bolsena is noted for its beautiful lake, but Toto would not enjoy time sipping wine on her shores. Instead she had to endure a very hot summer, a dark, bitterly cold winter, and inedible food. To add to her anguish, the other women prisoners regarded her with suspicion, and she was shunned.

The distinguished journalist William Rospigliosi, whose family boasted a 17th century pope, Clement the Ninth, was also arrested and taken to Bolsena. Later the Rome and Vatican correspondent of Time magazine recalled: 'Conditions of detention in Bolsena were particularly appalling and furthermore some of the locals objected to the presence of what they called "an enemy of Italy and Germany" in their village. They put pressure on the authorities and Miss Koopman was sent to another detention camp[28] in the same area.'

Throughout her life Toto had relished the company of fascinating, sometimes quite mad people, and had been both entertained and highly entertaining. Now she sat for hours on end, day after day, in squalor and loneliness and fear, only relieved by occasional visits from Elizabeth Eichmann who had avoided capture, despite her sympathies but possibly due to being German.

*

Dressed in her finest, dining on the finest, Coco Chanel wafted in and out of the Ritz and her apartment awaiting the return of von Dincklage…who had flown to Berlin for an appointment with Goebbels, the sinister Minister for Propaganda, and the Fuhrer himself, Adolf Hitler.

---

[28] The location of which is unknown.

CHAPTER 13

AGENT WESTMINSTER

'They hate one another and delight in undoing the other's arrangements.'
– Coco Chanel to diplomat Brian Wallace

Dincklage returned to Paris, and Chanel. It was clear he was rather pleased with himself to have been invited to an audience with Hitler, the man he had once dismissed as an 'upstart'. Henceforth, he would work directly with Berlin – something he considered a great honour. He journeyed to Germany with Baron Louis de Vaufreland, an openly and flamboyantly gay Frenchman who was an Abwehr agent – agent number F-7667, with the code name Piscatory – who, despite the Fuhrer's persecution of homosexuals, thrived under the Nazi leadership. The newly elevated Dincklage immediately arranged for Vaufreland to meet Chanel at the Ritz – where else? – where the Frenchman said he would secure the freedom of her nephew Andre, and wrest back control of her perfume business from the hated Wertheimers. In return? She would become a valued Nazi agent, using her powerful contacts in Spain, Paris and, the greatest prize of all, London, where Winston Churchill, her admirer and friend, was now prime minister.

And so Coco became Agent F-7124, codename Agent Westminster.[29] They made an unlikely duo: one in his early 30s, pudgy, effete and, as one Free French report described Vaufreland, 'highly dangerous'; the other a petite, still boyish-figured fashion designer, albeit a rather successful one, in her late 50s who knew nothing of the business of spying. The common bond was their anti-Semitism – that and the conviction that soon all of Europe would be under Hitler's control. In other words, they had joined what they believed would be the winning side.

The pair were run by an Abwehr lieutenant named Hermann Neubauer (later to work for the Americans after the war), who met Chanel at her boutique and accepted her rather vague suggestion that she should go to Madrid and London 'to give her important friends economic and political information'. Cynics might think she just fancied a break from Paris – which she did – rather in the way that, years later, it became the habit of enterprising newspaper reporters in need of an all-expenses-paid week on a beach to inform their news editors that they had had it on best authority that Lord

---

[29] Chanel later denied the name was chosen by her as a reference to her former lover Bendor. Maybe it was the choice of her Nazi handlers, thus acknowledging the duke's true allegiance.

Lucan had turned up in some hot and pleasant place in the world…

In August 1941, Chanel and Vaufreland left by train for Madrid, where she booked into the Ritz and he stayed with the Spanish branch of his aristocratic family. Her priority seemed to be the improvement of the sales of No 5 in Spain, however, as on her first day in the Spanish capital she headed straight for the Chanel office.

On 13th August, she and Vaufreland sat down to dinner with, among other guests, a British diplomat named Brian Wallace and his wife. Wallace's report to London makes fascinating, if confusing, reading. He prefaced his remarks by saying that Chanel is 'a friend of the PM' and 'impressed me deeply with her sincerity'. He then went on to say that Chanel had said that the Germans in Paris 'are bitterly anti-French but have a great admiration for all that is British.' She also talked of a 'great lack of co-ordination between the Nazi civil and military authorities', and concluded, 'They hate one another and delight in undoing the other's arrangements. They are all frightened, they are all wretched, and the watchers are themselves being watched.'

So what was she up to? It was probably her way of trying to convince Britain that she was really on their side and could be trusted as a go-between, all the while emphasising the admiration, and things in common, that Germany allegedly had with Britain.

When Chanel and Vaufreland returned to Paris after three weeks she heard that nephew Andre had been returned from his PoW camp, free but ill. With that matter attended to, she had a further obsession: she would now turn her efforts to ensuring the Wertheimers were stripped of their controlling shareholding in Chanel Parfums. But how? This was how: under Nazi laws outlawing Jewish ownership of businesses.

What a busy girl she was…

CHAPTER 14

FOR THE WANT OF AIRCRAFT

'This was his hour. His personal force and genius [...] swept aside many obstacles.'
— Winston Churchill

Her once fine clothes torn, dirty and hanging off her, Toto had not seen a bar of soap never mind a bottle of perfume for months. Surviving on mouthfuls of disgusting food, ignored and bored, remarkably she still displayed great dignity and poise, and was determined her spirit would not be beaten. Then, for no apparent reason – or at least not one she was told – she was moved to the Massa Martana detention camp in Perugia, 40 miles to the west of Bolsena, and her life would take another turn due to one man's standing up for both his convictions and his concerns.

Beaverbrook had been very wary of war and had favoured a negotiation with Hitler, and even thought he could have achieved it, given the chance. He shared that view with the Duke of Windsor and Joseph Kennedy,

US ambassador to London and father of the future president, and, as a result, was viewed with suspicion by some of Chamberlain's cabinet. All that changed, however, when Hitler invaded a neutral Norway in April 1940. What may have been considered until that point as a 'phony war' was over and, as far as Beaverbrook was concerned, there was only one man to steer Britain to victory: his greatest friend and ally, Winston Churchill. He immediately sent a note to Churchill, urging him to take over as prime minister should Chamberlain fall which, by then, seemed inevitable. He also begged him not to serve under Chamberlain's preferred choice as successor, Lord Halifax.

Churchill said he would not stake his own claim, but if asked to serve under Halifax he would say nothing. When Churchill, Halifax and Chamberlain met to discuss the formation of a government of national unity, the prime minister implied that the Labour Party would not join if it meant serving under Churchill. Halifax therefore was the only real choice. True to his word, Winston said nothing and, according to Churchill, there followed a silence which lasted for two minutes. As Beaverbrook later wrote: 'It was the silence that saved Britain', and Winston Churchill became the new leader of the country at war. And his first and only choice as minister of aircraft production? The Beaver himself.

But Beaverbrook had a powerful enemy: the king. George VI disliked the man primarily because of his support of the Duke of Windsor and his role in the abdication crisis, but also because he was not really trusted in his native Canada, a legacy from some of his dodgier deals as a young man on his way to his first million. Churchill was firm, however, and was determined to take aircraft production from the Air Ministry and hand it to his old friend. He knew that only Beaverbrook could – and would – shred the red tape that strangled Whitehall.

Overnight, Stornoway House was transformed into the new Ministry of Aircraft Production, and three favoured Express journalists were plucked from the iconic 'Black Lubyanka' offices in Fleet Street and planted in a top floor bedroom of Stornoway to help with planning and propaganda. A fourth, and his most inspired choice, was to lure Patrick Hennessy, the Irish-born general manager of Ford in Dagenham. His job was the key to Beaverbrook's success: finding materials, particularly aluminium and magnesium. The results were astonishing. The Beaver insisted that aircraft should take priority over all other types of munitions, and the figures show just how successful he was: barely 8,000 planes were produced in 1939, whereas a year later that total had almost doubled to more than 15,000; the following year it was more than 20,000. Production continued to increase steadily throughout the war. Britain, it is certain, would not have won the Battle of Britain without the Spitfires and Hurricanes that were rolling off the assembly lines at such an increased rate.

Manufacture of both planes was moved from the Southampton factories which, located on England's south coast, were an easy target for the Luftwaffe and had already been badly damaged. Instead, the Beaver decentralised manufacture to bus depots, barns – anywhere that would not be spotted by enemy planes. When he rang Lord Nuffield to ask why his Morris Motors factory at Castle Bromwich in the Midlands was producing nothing, Nuffield blamed government red tape and sarcastically suggested that he might like to 'take control'. 'That's very kind of you,' Beaverbrook replied, and hung up. And immediately took control.

On another occasion, the Beaver rang Sir Charles Craven, head of Vickers, which was manufacturing Spitfires. Craven, he was told, was 'indisposed', and when the Vickers boss called him back, he explained he had in fact been in the lavatory. Beaver was much amused at the observation: 'I can only deal with one shit at a time.'

True to form, Beaverbrook did things his way…and that way bore absolutely no resemblance whatsoever to the strict regulations of the Air Ministry which, he had insisted, played no part in this great new venture. Management was conducted by telephone or in person; memos in triplicate were a thing of the past, and few records were kept. (How Whitehall must have hated that!) He grabbed control of aircraft repairs as well as production, and German-Jewish engineers, interned in Britain as enemy aliens, were put to work in the factories. Then came his celebrated appeal for the country to give up their pots and pans for the war effort. An appeal for funding was launched throughout the whole of the UK, and all newspapers ran pictures of children going from house to house collecting utensils in prams. The Women's Voluntary Service co-ordinated the project, which involved 1,600 collection centres, and the Beaver proclaimed: 'We want your metal and we want it now! We will turn your pots and pans into Spitfires and Hurricanes, Blenheims and Wellingtons!' It was vintage Beaverbrook.

He also launched the Spitfire Fund, which soon brought in £1 million a month, and greatly boosted the morale of the country, alone in its fight against Hitler. Churchill's private secretary Jock Colville wrote in his diary on 13th June 1940: 'It is Winston and Beaverbrook who have really galvanised the country.'

Time Magazine said in a cover story: 'Even if Britain goes down this fall, it will not be Lord Beaverbrook's fault. If she holds out, it will be his triumph.'

And Churchill himself, in his memoirs, wrote: 'During these weeks of intense struggle and ceaseless anxiety, Lord Beaverbrook rendered a single service. This was his hour. His personal force and genius [...] swept aside many obstacles.'

Beaverbrook's vintage had worked like magic, and the rate at which fighters were being produced in the run-up to the Battle of Britain was two and a half times that of Germany. His success, and particularly his buccaneering methods, enraged several Cabinet colleagues and Service chiefs who called him a 'pirate' and 'highwayman' for seizing supplies of the raw materials they wanted.

But Air Chief Marshal Lord Dowding of the RAF

was right when he said later: 'It was the difference between victory and defeat.'

Though Beaverbrook was triumphant there were other great concerns to occupy his mind. The first was Churchill's mood swings – his 'black dog' depressions as he called them – and the Beaver was determined to help his friend through these bleak phases.

This was never truer than after the fall of France, when Britain feared the Germans would be greatly aided if they got their hands on the French fleet. Such an acquisition would mean a powerful addition to their own navy, and had to be averted at all costs. The War Cabinet agonised at length on what to do. Negotiations between Britain and France to keep the fleet away from the Nazis had failed, and so the terrible question of whether to bomb the fleet was put to the Cabinet. The most powerful French warships were anchored off Mers-el-Kebir in French Algeria, and Churchill knew what had to be done but could not bring himself to do it. After seemingly endless ministerial debate, Churchill asked Beaverbrook, and Beaverbrook alone, to accompany him into the Downing Street garden. The two men walked in silence for a moment, then almost broke into a trot. In the end it was Beaverbrook who said, 'Winston, the only way, however we may hate it, is to disable those ships and there is only one way to secure that end.'

At 5.54pm on 3rd July 1940, British warships and planes struck, with a follow-up action five days later. The most powerful part of the French fleet was destroyed, but at great cost: close on 1,300 French sailors perished, and Churchill wrote, 'This was the most hateful decision, the most unnatural and painful in which I have ever been concerned.' He might never have made it but for Beaverbrook, and it vividly illustrates the strength of the bond between the two men. Both had flaws galore, but a lack of courage was not one of them.

The second concern on the Beaver's mind was the safety of his son Max. Despite their previous hostilities over Toto, father and son cared deeply for each other. The Beaver had tried – and failed – to have Max grounded to a supervisory role, but Wing Commander, the Hon Maxwell Aitken DSO, was having none of it. He was a fighter pilot with at least 14 'kills' to his name. Terra firma was the place to be when playing golf or in bed with a pretty girl; the sky was his happy hunting ground.

Typical of the old man's concern was this telegram:

'To Wing Cdr Max Aitken, RAF Headquarters, Cairo. Give me news of your health and tell me about yourself.'

Happily, the news was that he was alive and well, and although officially non-operational with No 46 Squadron in the Middle East, he still managed to shoot down two Junkers from his Bristol Beaufighter. Max was made for war in the air; but he dismissed the rather romantic notion that British and German pilots had a shared gallantry. 'Nonsense,' he said, 'I hated them, I just wanted to kill as many as I could before they could kill me or my friends.'

The third worry for Beaverbrook was none other than Toto. Though they had fallen out spectacularly in 1935, he wished her no ill, and especially at the hands of the enemy. In fact he greatly admired her courage, and regretted the way he had treated her. By the spring of 1941 he knew she must have been captured – or worse – because she was no longer sending messages back to the Radio Shack, and all British Intelligence sources had was that she had been arrested in the mountains near Florence. It seems hard to grasp, but for two whole years neither Max nor he knew of her fate.

On 25th July 1943 Mussolini was overthrown and, on the order of Italy's monarch, King Victor Emmanuel III, he was arrested. The new government signed an armistice with the Allies on 8th September and, simultaneously, most political prisoners were freed, many of whom went straight back to fighting for the Italian Resistance against the Germans who were now in Italy, no longer as an ally but as an enemy. Most of the partisan fighters thought – rightly as it turned out – that the Italian army would put up 'little opposition' to their new enemy, so they would have to do it for them. They saw themselves as crusaders, out to rid their country of the Nazis but also its shameful Fascist past. There could be no going back. From the underground newspaper l'Italia Libera, the cry went out: '*Hunt down the Germans! Sabotage the railways! Above all, never allow yourselves to be discouraged*!' Stirring stuff. Even

Beaverbrook, the mighty propagandist, would have been hard pressed to do better.

Never was there a greater cause. The German occupiers and their Fascist followers were engaged in some of the worst savagery of the war, especially when Rome was liberated by the Allies in June 1944. As German divisions made their slow retreat northwards, and the partisans, emboldened by what appeared to be certain defeat for the Nazis and by the encouragement of the Allied Commander General Alexander to rise up, the SS and the Wehrmacht committed a series of atrocities against the Resistance and non-fighting Italians. No mercy was shown and Hitler, ever more vengeful and madder by the day, ordered: 'They must be massacred, killed, annihilated!'

The attack on Civitella in the Val di Chiana is remembered to this day. When the troops reached this beautiful medieval walled town they looted the place of alcohol and spent the day drinking themselves to a frenzy. When, in the evening, four partisans attacked, a gun battle broke out, and the following dawn, despite debilitating hangovers, the inhabitants of Civitella were rounded up and taken to a wood and questioned in the hope that the partisans would be given up. In vain.

Two days later, buildings were set ablaze, and innocent men, women and children were herded into the market square and machine gunned. Their bodies were thrown into the flames.

In Caprara, three girls were tied to a tree and stakes

were pushed through their bodies.

In Marzabotto in the Appenines, no fewer than 900 people, including 155 children and five priests, were massacred.

There were many stories of outstanding bravery, however. One woman called Cleonice Tomassetti, one of 43 rounded up but the only woman, was made to walk three miles with the men around her to their execution. As they were about to die, she called out to her compatriots: 'Don't be afraid. Remember, it is better to die as Italians than to live as spies and servants of the Germans.'

It was *this* that Toto had been fighting; *this* that had so fired her courage. But it would be much later before she learned of the atrocities and what the enemy had been capable of.

When Mussolini was overthrown, Toto was not one of the prisoners released. But in the general confusion, and as the Fascists were planning to hand the remaining inmates to Germany to be taken to Hitler's concentration camps, she escaped the camp at Massa Martana…though 'escaped' does not accurately describe what happened. Such was the chaos, that she simply walked through the gates without being stopped, and kept walking straight for the Monti Martani mountains, 30 miles south in Perugia. There she joined a disparate group, which included an engineer, three former soldiers who had brought their weapons with them, two Jewish men, one of whom had been the village tailor-cum-barber, and several farm labourers.

Her friend and admirer, the journalist William

Rospigliosi said: 'She was not immediately liberated but managed to take refuge in the mountains. Other war prisoners soon joined them. I was able to flee Perugia thanks to a network she put into place. Many escaped the Germans thanks to her.'

As soon as she was able, Toto was back on the airwaves to Cherkley, much to the immense relief of Beaverbrook, Max, and both Churchills, father and son. Max got the news to her brother Ody, and the word soon spread.

Toto, however, learned that her father had died two years earlier in Holland, at the age of 63. In view of that sad news, and given that she was in serious need of rest and recovery, she could have seized the opportunity to try to flee to somewhere safe, the US maybe, or even the British countryside, for the most part untroubled by German bombs; somewhere with a proper bed, a bath, and proper food. Instead, though severely weakened, she went straight back to working with the Resistance. As she explained to Laura Aitken:

> *'It was simple. Call it unfinished business if you like, but I was determined to carry on fighting for what was right. You couldn't live through those times without feeling burning anger and the need to do anything, absolutely anything, to get rid of Hitler and all the evil he stood for. I felt that I would be letting down everyone if I had opted for an easy time; the Partisans had been very good to me, and it would*

have been letting down friends if I had run away. I suppose I might have made a different decision if I had known what was in store for me, but even then I doubt if I would have. I felt somehow a bit safer – though of course I wasn't – by being able to get messages out to Cherkley now and then.

At one point I was the only woman with 250 men. They were made up of so many factions; monarchists, communists, escaped PoWs, some of them Yugoslav, two of them Russian and a lone Scotsman called Stuart Hood[30], who had been an Intelligence officer before he was captured in the North African campaign. Unfortunately, he moved on before we had got to know each other.

What saddened me most was the death of my father. He had died without my knowing while I was locked up. In a strange way, I felt guilty that I was not able to see him. It affected me badly.'

An Olympic showjumper she may not have become, but without a doubt her father would have been proud of his only daughter.

Most nights she slept outside under a blanket on the ground, and attended to her needs behind a tree or bush when the men were asleep. After several weeks, when it seemed the enemy had left the area, Toto and

---

[30] Stuart Hood went on to have a distinguished career in television as controller of BBC1, launching programmes such as Z Cars and That Was the Week That Was.

a handful of friends found safety and shelter in a village near Capodimonte on the shore of Lake Bolsena. They were welcomed by farming families, and benefitted from warmth and the sort of meals which, despite being basic, tasted like heaven after two years of foul-tasting prison food. Gradually she began to build up her strength and gained a little weight; and, with that, her vitality returned, as did her enthusiasm for life.

Thanks to the determination and intelligence of Emilio Lussu, and a dapper, earnest man of 51 named Cecil Roseberry, the Italy section of SOE was now active and ready to help the newly liberated Italians defeat the Germans. Their operations were mostly confined to the south of the country, but in late 1943 Toto met two SOE men, one English, the other Scottish, who had arrived by parachute a week before in Piedmont. Their Italian was mostly of the phrase book variety, so she was able to translate for them and draw some rudimentary maps. She recalls: *'I cannot remember their names, but we fed them for a day or so before they moved on. They were able to tell me some news from England, mostly about the royal family, which was of no great interest to me. But it was good to know that Britain was bearing up so well and that, at last, it had troops in Italy. We knew we were not alone.'*

It might have been so different an ending; indeed, so much worse but for one crucial event: The Battle of Britain. It had been won thanks in great part to Toto's former lover: Beaverbrook.

CHAPTER 15

HIDDEN IN PLAIN SIGHT

'It was dangerous, but in the end it really did appeal.'
— Toto

Toto was liked by the locals, and she trusted them. Some evenings she took part in their poker school, and in the daytime helped the children of two families learn English. The simple, good food, lots of sleep and the warmth — there was a plentiful supply of logs, so the fires burned long and hot, the stove was stoked, and the water in the tin bath warmed — saw colour return to her face and she felt stronger day by day. When she eventually moved on they gave her a card, made by the children, with their thanks written in English. '*I lost that card and it was one of my most treasured possessions,*' she told Laura Aitken. '*Even though I had never wanted children of my own, I loved my time with these three little girls and one boy*.'

News filtered through. Following Mussolini's arrest and Italy's switch to the Allies' side, British and US troops had a foothold in the south, but they were too far from

Toto and her Resistance fighters to be of any assistance. They carried on regardless.

But the country was still a broiling cauldron of factions: the Fascists supporting the Germans wanted the return of Mussolini; and the partisans were often made up of opposing groups, most notably the Communists and those who backed the king. In some cases, it was family against family, and the first task for the British SOE agents, who had at last been dropped into Italy, was to work out who were their friends and allies, and who were their enemies.

In the German-occupied parts, some of the fiercest resistance came from the women. In Turin, when the occupiers were rounding up Italian soldiers (their former allies) and marching them to prison camps, 500 of the cavalry soldiers were ordered to mount what horses were left and ride behind the column of their fellow prisoners. Word spread quickly, and within minutes hundreds of women arrived on the scene and hurled stones at the horses. They scattered in a riot of rearing, bucking panic – which conveniently separated the riders from their saddles – and the women pulled the bewildered men into doorways, and temporary safety. They were given civilian clothing and, arm in arm with the girls, they then walked nonchalantly to the railway station, looking for all the world like young lovers. When the train was clear of the city, it slowed to a crawl so the men could jump from the carriages into the countryside to join up with Resistance groups and fight another day. It was a well-organised ploy and an incredibly brave one.

As one of these women wrote later: 'It was thus that *our* war began.'

And war it certainly was. The Germans launched into their revenge, indiscriminately and viciously, and many women, young girls and female infants were shot dead. Far from deterring other women, however, they rose in swathes across Italy. The Italian author Natalia Ginzburg wrote: 'The small virtues of women – their skills at caring for others, their instant responsiveness – were suddenly becoming big.'

But massacre was not the only string to the bow of revenge. The Germans and Fascisti had another vile weapon throughout Italy: torture centres, where reports of the atrocities carried out within their walls were the stuff of darkest nightmares.

Toto's bravery, and that of the hundreds of other women who were joining the Resistance by the day, can never be overstated. They were spurred on to defend their land because, as one of their leaders declared, 'As the specific creator of life, a woman is more prone, even more than men, to defend it.' As a vital cog in the Resistance wheel, Toto personified that sisterhood, and thanks to her links with London her immediate band of fighters had been bolstered by a weapons drop and the arrival of a doctor and also a safe blower (recently released from jail) whose skills were put to excellent use when bridges needed to be destroyed.

Protected, and relatively safe in her farmhouse, Toto continued to liaise with her contacts in London and they with her, until the incident which even she, with all her reserves of moral and physical strengths, could not have prepared for.

On the night of 22nd June 1944, a Sicilian tried to steal a truck that the Resistance fighters had hidden in the woods near the farmhouse where Toto was sleeping. He was a thief, pure and simple, and he wanted the vehicle as transport for himself. He was caught by her colleagues, and badly beaten but not killed. But the partisans' leniency was their undoing. The incensed man reported the incident to local Fascists, who still had a stranglehold in the area, and Toto and her friends were rounded up in a raid in the middle of the night two days later. She was driven back to jail, and hurled into a small, damp, stinking cell. She had no change of clothes, not even a toothbrush.

At daybreak, a gang of Blackshirts, some very drunk, arrived at the jail and ordered her, at gunpoint, to go outside to a courtyard where she was consumed with dread. *'They were disgusting, very drunk and very smelly,'* she recalled. *'I was convinced they would brutalise me and frankly, I would rather be killed than that.'*

She was saved by the arrival of a Blackshirt officer, who restored order by shooting in the air. With his blond hair and blue eyes, it was obvious he was not Italian and at first Toto thought he might be German. He apologised profusely for the behaviour of his men. 'The boys are very agitated because we are about to stage a trap for members of the Resistance and there will be some violent fighting,' he explained. Then he took her aside and told her, 'I am British, I am on your side. I'm with the Secret Intelligence Service.' She didn't believe a word of it, but replied, 'In that case, tell me the news from England and get me out of here.'

No news was forthcoming.

Later that morning he returned and her heart sank. 'Kiss me,' he said, and when she accused him of being no better than the men whose antics he had broken up earlier, he was again filled with remorse and promised to come back and secure her release. She wasn't exactly filled with hope, and when one of her friends from the village, the daughter of an innkeeper, brought some food to the jail, she learned the truth: her blond 'saviour' was just another Fascist, and a senior one. Then more devastating news: the leader of their group of fighters had been killed by his captors that morning. Toto was distraught: *'It upset me much more than I had expected. Our little band had lived like siblings for four months, shared all our experiences, knew all about each other. We sang together, talked about our families and our childhoods. The man who died, though I remember him only as Georgio, was funny as well as brave. His death shattered me and I wept very much. I kept thinking, are we really achieving anything to justify all this killing?'*

Later that evening, the blue-eyed man did indeed return, with two Blackshirts. This time he offered to drive her to a hotel in Foligno, Perugia, thought to be the

Italia. Fearing a trap, she nevertheless agreed. When they arrived, she discovered that the hotel had been turned into a temporary jail. But it was an improvement on the filthy cell she had spent the last sleepless, fearful night in, and for that she was grateful. There was little else to be thankful for. Guards were stationed inside and outside the building, and she was only allowed to leave her room for one hour a day, accompanied by armed guards, for communal exercise on a small terrace.

She was kept there for four weeks, her only hope resting on the advance of the Allies who she believed were still slowly working their way north. Then came an unexpected visit: an Italian, in a paratrooper's uniform, came to her requesting help. Like the previous fraudster, he claimed to work for British SIS, and even showed her a photograph of a man he claimed was a dangerous anti-Fascist. He told her it was his job to track him down and return him to Rome. But why would SIS want to arrest an anti-Fascist? It made no sense to Toto, and she did not recognise the man, or the woman in the picture, who was apparently his Greek mistress. But she decided to play along. She engaged with her visitor, who admitted that the man with the blue eyes who had previously tried to kiss her was born in England, to a Norwegian mother and Italian father, and was a dyed-in-the-wool Fascist. He had pretended the save her life, and might have got away with it had he not tried to seduce her so crudely.

There was more than an element of farce to the Fascist's strategy, and it failed completely, so much so that, looking back 36 years later, Toto couldn't help but laugh at the memory of it: *'I persuaded this nice young man to tell the jailers that he was taking me with him back to Rome. Once outside, by then great friends, he shook my hand. I gave him a little peck on the cheek and we parted. I never knew what happened to him and only hoped he wasn't punished for his kindness.'*

Toto now had to weigh up a hefty dilemma: she had worked against the Nazis and the Fascists in one capacity or another for almost nine years. For the last three she had either been in filthy prison cells without proper food, or in the woods and mountains living with the constant fear of being caught, hearing that knock on the door – on the occasions when there was a door to knock – that meant she had been discovered. She had been brave and determined, and she was in no doubt that she had picked the right cause. But maybe it was time to seek safety and comfort before she was caught again, because who knew what the outcome of that 'next time' would be…

She told Laura Aitken:

'I was really exhausted and constantly looking over my shoulders. I didn't want to give up because I knew we were right and if nobody fought, if people just turned their backs and walked away, I believed the world would be plunged into a new dark age. I may have been frail from it all, but I couldn't desert my friends, my comrades. I had really grown to love and admire them. So I compromised. I knew my friend Elizabeth Eichmann was in Venice so I thought if I went there for a while, I could build up my strength before returning to help the Resistance. Even then, I felt guilty because I knew my friends didn't have the luxury of that choice.'

With the help of those friends and comrades, Toto began the 250-mile journey to Venice, a city she knew well and adored. Today, this trip is a five-hour train ride to the north; in 1944, at the height of war, it took almost three days, an uncomfortable combination of foot, lorry, car, an old ambulance and then train – she turned down the offer of a donkey because she said, 'The poor thing looked in worse shape than me!' – each facilitated by the Resistance for whom Toto was very much regarded as the heroine for financing them as best she could, and for her ability to pass on and receive news from England. Finally, on the 4th September, she reached Venice and headed straight for the exquisite Danieli hotel near St Mark's Square, then (and still) the queen of Venetian hotels.

Shortly after Mussolini declared his support for Hitler in 1940, Churchill said ominously: 'People who go to Italy to look at ruins won't have to go as far as Naples and Pompeii in future.' As a result, the RAF bombed much of the country, but mercifully not Venice. The only time it came under sustained air attack was towards the end of the war with Operation Bowler when Venice harbour was precision bombed to cut off supplies to the Germans, a ploy which worked brilliantly. As a result the treasures of Venice remained remarkably unscathed, not least the Danieli.

Exhausted, ragged and hungry, she recalls:

'My friend Elizabeth Eichmann was staying there

in a suite. Her sister Ingerborg had gone elsewhere, though I'm not sure I knew where. Elizabeth's first job was to get me looking presentable, but I had another priority. I had to sleep and sleep and sleep after that journey. But after a day or two I felt so much better and we went clothes shopping. It wasn't easy in such bad times, and I was rather skinny, but we managed and we ate well, certainly a lot better than I was used to!'

For several days the two women simply enjoyed being together, relaxing as well as they could given that Italy was still at war. They walked, talked and ate, and Toto said, *'Elizabeth pampered me and listened endlessly to my stories. She must have been exhausted!'*

It gave Toto time for reflection on how brave her friends had been, especially in the early days of the German occupation when there was no help from Britain, no arms drops or money to buy weapons. They had been entirely on their own, living off the land and by their wits. She didn't know it then, of course, but long after the end of the war she read that 35,000 Resistance fighters and their supporters had died, and thousands had been sent to concentration camps. Had she known the terrible level of attrition, would she have changed her mind? Not a chance.

Her time at the Danieli was not all relaxation. The Germans were in the city, in force, and groups of soldiers were ordered to search hotels, guest houses, even restaurants for those they deemed enemies. The Danieli was searched almost nightly, though there is no reason to believe Toto was their sole objective. But she and Elizabeth (for harbouring her) were in great danger, and Toto decided she could not put her friend at risk any longer: she would return to the partisans in Perugia. Elizabeth, however, had another idea, and an audacious one at that: she would 'present' Toto to the most senior Nazi in the city.

When Hitler came to power he introduced a system of gauleiters – Nazi party faithfuls who administered districts throughout Germany – the most notorious of whom was Joseph Goebbels, on his way up the ladder to greater evil. As each country was conquered, the system was set up, and the gauleiter of Venice was a portly functionary named Albert Menkel, who was enjoying his '15 minutes of fame' in a beautiful city which was not being bombed by the Allies. His time in the city had passed with little incident and he had no desire for that to change. He was also not in Hitler's immediate thoughts – exactly the way he liked it.

Menkel was looking forward to dinner at the Danieli, at which he would be the guest of honour. He would wear his finest dress uniform and medals and act the VIP that, in his heart of hearts, he probably knew he was not. The dinner was being given by an Italian man, a friend of Elizabeth and a collector of Renaissance works who had made his fortune as an art dealer. Inviting Herr Gauleiter was a kind of insurance policy, should he ever need to make a claim on it, and together they came up with the plan that there would be no better disguise for Toto than to be hidden in plain sight.

On Friday 17th September, as soldiers once more searched the length and breadth of the Danieli for people or property that shouldn't be there, Miss Toto Koopman was thoroughly enjoying herself at a grand dinner in the Terrazza restaurant. For the duration of the night she was to be Baroness van Halmaell, the Belgian title she had adopted for fun while in Paris whilst trying to keep up with the Mdivanis, the phoney princelings.

And what better place for the beautiful baroness than to be seated at dinner next to Albert Menkel:

> *'I think this was Elizabeth's idea, and at first I was very much against it. But the more I thought about, the more I liked it. It was dangerous, but in the end it really did appeal. I told him I was from Belgium originally but had lived much of my life in Germany and had met von Ribbentrop and had had Nazi lovers. We spoke German throughout and he told me about the mission the week before in which Waffen-SS special forces had flown by gliders to rescue Mussolini from his captors in Imperatore. Nobody apart from the host and Elizabeth knew of the deception — that was absolutely vital — and afterwards the three of us went to the suite and laughed and laughed! I was feeling very elated by it but somewhere in the back of my mind I was sure it couldn't last. Looking back, I*

should have made sure that I had one of the Partisans forge my papers in the name of Halmaell but of course I hadn't thought of it then.'

Three days later, Toto was writing a letter and drinking coffee in a café near the Rialto. As she sat writing, two soldiers came in and asked everybody to stay where they were. When they saw the letter was in French they alerted an officer from outside, who began questioning Toto: Who are you? Why are you in Venice?

She replied forcefully in German: 'I am the Baroness van Halmaell.'

But a search of her bag revealed otherwise.

The visit, alone, to the coffee shop had been one gamble too many. Toto was arrested and thrown into a Kubelwagen, a Volkswagen-based small army truck, and taken for questioning.

CHAPTER 16

THIS HELL ON EARTH

'I would rather have been shot immediately than to endure this.'

– Toto

The SS officer questioning Toto was polite but firm. It took less than 30 minutes to establish the true identity of the 'baroness'. She remembered:

'He was old-fashioned in a very formal, Teutonic sort of way, the perfect gentleman, but I knew he had ice in his veins. I answered his questions honestly because it would have been pointless doing otherwise. But when he asked for names of my compatriots I made them up and said some had died. The only time my interrogator's face slipped was when I told him I had been sat next to the gauleiter at the Danieli. He laughed at that.'

At three in the afternoon, Toto was put in the back of a Mercedes staff car and driven 150 miles west to

Milan. They stopped at Verona to pick up a Gestapo officer who was, judging from the little conversation she could hear from the back seat, very senior in rank. It was unclear where they were taking her.

Elizabeth Eichmann had been questioned at the Danieli, but not arrested. Desperately worried about her friend, and despite her best efforts, no one would reveal Toto's whereabouts.

When they reached Milan, Toto was deposited at the station, surrounded by Jews, gypsies and prostitutes. She also noticed political captives, and a cold fear drained her face of all colour. They were herded onto a train. Amongst her fellow travellers were two heavily pregnant women, and young children, bewildered and tearful. They were transported north, to Berlin, a distance of 550 miles, and then crammed into a cattle truck 30 feet long and 10 feet wide. The final 56 miles took more than 10 hours, spent mostly standing up as they grappled for space. There was a single bucket to service their needs. No food or water was provided.

According to her friends, and Laura Aitken, Toto was happy to talk about her life if asked, though she rarely offered information otherwise. But when it came to Ravensbruck concentration camp, a veil would descend. Maybe it was her way, or nature's way; a defensive, protective mechanism that kicked in, not unusual, or surprising. Her only comment: *'I would rather have been shot immediately than to endure this.'* And this from a woman, so courageous and resilient.

Of those who were taken to Ravensbruck, the concentration camp used almost solely to incarcerate women, and the pride and joy of Heinrich Himmler, architect of the Holocaust, many never, ever spoke of their time in the camp, not even to the men they later married or to the children they bore. Some survived only to commit suicide, unable to live with the memories of the horrors they had endured. In the case of the Russian survivors, many were interrogated by the Communists on their return home, the Soviets suspecting them of collaboration with the Nazis. Several were tortured when they failed to convince the KGB of their innocence.

The reluctance to talk about what had been witnessed, and endured, in the camp, was coupled with a reluctance to listen too. The world had had enough; had closed its ears and eyes and wanted to move on. As a result, few people outside Germany heard about Ravensbruck until five decades later.

When it was first built in 1938, war had yet to be declared, but a programme of camp construction was underway as a central part of Hitler's 'cleansing' of his empire, ridding it of Judaism once and for all. In those early days, new arrivals thought they had been sent to a holiday camp. It was set in the Mecklenberg forest, on part of Himmler's country estate, and a glance through the trees revealed a church spire, a sparkling lake bordered with boat houses, and an orchard and flowerbeds planted with rich-red salvias. This postcard-ready picture was complete with gooseberry bushes, linden trees, chicken coops and rabbit hutches. (All that was missing were children, blond-haired, blue eyed and rosy-cheeked; good little Aryans singing their praises to the Fuhrer and the Fatherland…)

One early Ravensbruck prisoner was a German Communist, Margarete Buber-Neumann, who described her first impressions: 'I looked across the great square and could not believe my eyes. It was surrounded by manicured lawns, covered by flowerbeds. A wide street bordered by young trees…the square and the streets seemed freshly raked. I saw a white wooden barrack and beside it a large cage, the size of a birdhouse, like you see at a zoo. Within it paraded peacocks, and on a climbing tree dangled monkeys and a parrot which always screamed the same word: 'Mama'. I wondered: This is a concentration camp?'

Early inmates were served porridge and dried fruit and nuts, along with bread, margarine and sausage. At the outset, Ravensbruck housed just 900 women; in 1944 there were close to 20,000, it is rumoured, with the resultant appalling conditions and food.

By the time Toto arrived as a guest of the Third Reich, as prisoner No 77370, she was already in a weak state physically from previous incarcerations, and barely recovered despite the rest and recuperation in Venice. Imprisonment in Italy had been wretched, but what Toto was confronted with now was beyond human imagination. The women were ordered to wait in line to be 'processed'. The guards then yelled 'Schnell! Schnell!'

('Quick! Quick!') as they were ordered to strip, and 'Yes, everything OFF! Strip, strip!' as possessions, however meagre or valuable, went into a brown paper bag. Their hair was checked for lice and then washed, but not as a courtesy: they were then shaved, and every strand of hair, long or short, was removed to the scalp, along with pubic hair. Later they would notice the signs posted all around the camp in several languages: 'Lice = Death'.

Each woman was given a plate, bowl, aluminium cup, knife, fork, spoon and a cloth for washing and drying utensils. Then came a toothbrush, tooth mug, a nugget of soap and a small towel. Finally, each was given a coloured triangle to be stitched onto their blue and white striped thin cotton dresses, which signified the category to which they belonged. Toto was given a red triangle, worn by those classified as 'political prisoners', and also bore the letter N, signifying *Niederllanderin*, or Dutch. The Jewish women wore two inverted triangles, the Star of David.

Birth and class were irrelevant. Elizabeth de Rothschild of Europe's most prominent banking family died in Toto's arms at the camp; a 25-year-old French princess, Anne de Bauffremont-Courtenay, was another victim. There were several Polish countesses, and those who had lived a genteel, privileged life before they had been sent to this hell on earth. They met their death alongside prostitutes, Jehovah's Witnesses who proclaimed that Hitler – and they were not exaggerating – was 'the Anti-Christ', lesbians, beggars, thieves, the insane, gypsies, spies, and tens of thousands of innocent Poles and Russians – grandmothers, mothers, sisters, children – who were guilty only of being from another country.

The total number of deaths at Ravensbruck will never be known, because when the Nazis knew their evil game was up they burned all the records and killed as many prisoners as they could before making their escape. But it is said that 132,000 women were incarcerated in the camp over six years, and it is believed that more than half of them died from disease, starvation or overwork. Others were shot, hanged, or put in the gas chambers which were eventually built by male prisoners from the nearby Lichtenburg camp. Some simply curled up and died of despair. In the last year of its existence, at least 80 women were killed each and every day.

One survivor I spoke to, the remarkable Mala Tribich MBE, arrived at the camp as 14-year-old Mala Helfgott from a Polish slave labour camp in November 1944. Her parents and most of the wider family were murdered by the Nazis. She did not realise until after the end of the war that her brother Ben had survived Buchenwald and was in England. He later captained the British weightlifting team at the 1956 and 1960 Olympics and was knighted in 2018. Mala spends much of her time talking to schoolchildren and other groups in the United Kingdom about the Holocaust and the lessons we must still learn from it.

She recalled:

'When the Germans invaded Poland, first I was put in the Jewish ghetto and then a slave labour camp. When we were rounded up and sent to Ravensbruck I was with my cousin Ann[31] who was three years younger and I was trying to look after her.

We didn't know where we were going when we left our labour camp. In fact I think the German guards were not sure either, because they kept receiving different orders. When we finally arrived, after four and a half days in a cattle truck, we were lined up at the train station and made to march in two columns, four people wide, clutching our few belongings in little bundles. Then we had to give all our details to the camp officials and hand over everything we had before we were stripped, shaved of all our hair, and made to take a freezing cold shower. There was no soap.

Then we walked out in columns, again lined by soldiers, and my memory is of my embarrassment when one soldier looked me up and down in a leering fashion. Then we were given those striped shifts and awful clogs which didn't fit. The worst thing was we no longer recognised each other, we were stripped of our personality, and when you lose your personality you lose all hope and you give up.

Ann and I were taken to the children's part of the camp so we were not forced into the sort of hard manual labour that killed so many of the women

---

[31] Ann survived and emigrated to Australia.

*there. You learned to be wise at the camp; for instance,
it was always best to be last in the queue for soup
because the vats of the stuff were never stirred. That
meant that the first in the queue got what was really
water, whereas getting the last of it at least gave some
nutrition, not much but a bit.'*

Mala added this terrible postscript: '*We were transferred
to Bergen-Belsen after 10 weeks and, compared with that place,
Ravensbruck at least seemed to be organised. My abiding memory
of Belsen is that I was constantly stepping over dead bodies.'*

Organised or not, the Ravensbruck guards revelled
in the killing, none more so than the chief guard Dorothea
Binz, known to all as 'the Beautiful Beast', and always
clad in a black cape which would flow behind her when
she rode her bicycle. One of the most horrific stories told
about her, appalling even by the satanic depths of the
Nazis, was how she encouraged those under her to throw
the prisoners' babies in the air and shoot them like some
sort of unimaginable fairground sideshow.

One Russian prisoner wrote a poem about the
merciless Binz:

*A beautiful blonde, you are so beautiful, with shining
blue eyes and locks of hair.
But if we could, we would tear the insides of
your soul and strangle your bloodthirsty heart.
Do you remember the girl you were whipping,
Jacqueline?*

How you stamped on Wanda, the Polish girl?
How you tortured the Russian girl Veronicka?
You and the dog…'

Shorn of her lustrous dark hair, dressed to face the icy German winter in just a thin striped shift dress, and frightened and in shock at the horrors of her surroundings, stood Miss Catharina 'Toto' Koopman, two weeks short of her 36th birthday. Once a celebrated Vogue model, the beautiful, mysterious toast of high society, and so brave and determined in the face of war, she was lost.

Where was the all-powerful Beaver, and where was her gallant Max? the Churchills? her darling Daddy? For the first time in her life she had no idea how − or even if − she would survive.

CHAPTER 17

MEANWHILE AT THE RITZ

Chanel, 'the horizontal collaborator'…

— the Free French

The Vichy government had adopted all of the Third Reich's laws against Jews 'and other vermin', and throughout France thousands had been rounded up and deported to Germany's extermination camps as part of the Final Solution. Just a 15-minute stroll from the Ritz, the Paris Jewish Quarter was eerily quiet, its residents either already dead, waiting to die in a German gas chamber, or soon to be deported. Chanel knew this and was undisturbed in that knowledge. All she really cared about was getting control back of La Societe des Parfums Chanel from those horrible, greedy Jews, the Wertheimers.

She had friends in high places, as the freeing of her nephew Andre had proved, so now she set about solving the 'Wertheimer problem'. Vaufreland contacted his aristocratic friend Prince Ernst Ratibor-Corvey, who in turn arranged for Chanel to meet Dr Kurt Blanke, the Nazi enforcer of the confiscation of Jewish property. He had already been highly successful in his endeavours and Chanel felt sure she was in good hands. Confident, she also wrote to the new Vichy government: 'Parfums Chanel is still the property of Jews and has been legally "abandoned" by the owners. I have an indisputable right of priority. The profits that I have received from my creations since the foundation of this business are disproportionate.'

There was one snag, however: the Wertheimers, reading the runes as early as the late 1930s, had been making arrangements to emigrate to the United States. But before they could do that, they made a secret deal with a wealthy non-Jew from Normandy, Felix Amiot, to hold the Chanel company in trust for them. In other words, the firm would no longer be a Jewish concern and therefore safe from the Aryanisation laws. With that safely negotiated, Pierre and Paul set sail with their families on the *SS Argentina* for their new lives in Manhattan. To make matters worse, once in New York they launched a new Bourjois scent appropriately named Courage, which was a bestseller, and began manufacture of No 5 at their new plant in Hoboken, New Jersey.

This entailed getting the secret formula for No 5 and its one vital ingredient, the type of jasmine found only in Grasse in the South of France. This was accomplished through an extraordinary James Bond-style operation by a man named Gregory Thomas, six feet eight inches tall and a US citizen educated at Cambridge, the Sorbonne and in Spain. Using his skills as a lawyer and as an agent for the Office of Strategic Services, the forerunner of the CIA, Thomas went to France loaded with Louis d'Or coins worth up to £3,000 each (in today's values) and bribed his way to the formula for No 5. He returned to New York and his paymasters, the Wertheimers, with large quantities of the crucial jasmine – and the all-important formula. For his troubles, Thomas found his bank account bolstered by £20 million (today's money), transferred by the Wertheimers.

To underline their success – and to rub salt into Chanel's weeping wounds – the brothers were early financial supporters of de Gaulle's Free French.

Mademoiselle Chanel was not happy. And events were soon to get much worse for the irate woman.

British and US forces, having entered the war, and led by the future president General Dwight Eisenhower, secured the beaches of Algeria and Morocco, both French territories. Churchill marked the occasion by broadcasting to Europe on the BBC: *'Now is not the end. It is not even the beginning of the end. But it is perhaps the end of the beginning.'*

Nicknamed *'une collaborateur horizontal'* (the horizontal collaborator) by the Free French, for reasons that do not require an explanation, Chanel listened in horror. And then the influential American magazine Life published a list of the guilty, which included her lawyer Rene de Chambrun. Life warned: 'Some collaborators will be assassinated […] others will be tried when France is free.'

In Paris the situation was turning increasingly ugly for German occupiers. Parisians had started turning their backs on them as they marched by. A senior Nazi told Berlin: 'There is a general rejection of all things German.' Worse still, General de Gaulle's Free French snipers were picking off some of the Nazi troops after the evening curfew fell.

In her suite at the Ritz, Chanel and Dincklage worried what was to come next and, in particular – obviously – what was to become of them. Her outrageous views were well known to de Gaulle: her remark at a lunch party that 'France has got what she deserves' had been recorded by his agents, and he was not likely to forgive or forget…

CHAPTER 18

NOT FIT FOR THE MASTER RACE

'Did I want to survive if this was the life I had to endure?'

— Toto

Toto was sent to Block 16. On her way she passed the remains of a woman's body, fused to the electrified fence. She was skeletal and had been shot in her pathetic effort to escape over the wire. As was the practice, the corpse had been left as a reminder to other possible escapees: Don't bother.

Beds were three layers of bunks with a base of wooden planks and mattresses filled with wood shavings. A thin checked white and blue blanket had been provided but would prove utterly inadequate against the bitter cold. Glancing around, it was clear there were not enough bunks for everyone, and the emaciated women were sleeping three or four to a mattress. Some were on the freezing concrete floor, covered in excrement. Many of them had no blanket at all.

Many of the women were sick, suffering from pneumonia, diarrhoea, gangrene or frostbite. Typhus was sweeping through the camp, too. If not sick, it was clear they were severely malnourished and exhausted from hard labour.[32] Favoured prisoners, those chosen for their skills as doctors or nurses or even secretaries, worked in the camp hospital or office block. They were still prisoners, however, and were shown no other favours.

Toto, not yet recovered from her time in jail, shook with the sheer horror of what she saw and heard: the ravaged bodies, many of them already dead but not removed to the mass burial pits; buckets overflowing with excreta, vomit and menstrual blood; rats that ran everywhere spreading their filth; the screech of machine gun fire outside; the screams of the women being shot. She later heard that lethal injections of poison took too long, and the gas chamber was not yet finished, so a firing squad had become the quickest, most efficient form of extermination until it was ready. But worst of all were the children, eyes and bones protruding, barely alive, clinging to their mothers.

Toto quickly learned that just because the women were in this hell all together, it did not mean they were friends or allies. It was a case of every wretch for herself and, if they had any energy left, they would fight,

---

[32] The order went out, in 1943, that too many women were dying at the camp, and it was vital they stayed alive in order to be able to work. 'Only the mad or sick should die,' Reichsfuhrer Himmler pronounced.

viciously, over the last scraps of food or drops of water. They all knew who the real enemy was, however, and if someone returned to their block after a beating, her block-mates would go to her.

Every single woman, if not defeated and simply waiting for blessed death, were fighting for their very lives.

Weeping was as commonplace as breathing.

Toto's arrival coincided with thousands of Jewish women from Hungary. They were among the final purge of the remaining Jews in the country, and by the end of the year 430,000 of Hungary's 750,000 Jewish had been sent to Hitler's camps, where many of them were exterminated. But because their homeland had been bombed so badly, train journeys were now not possible, so much of the 200-mile trip to the border had to be made on foot, no matter how frail or old or young the prisoner. As a result, many of the women who made it to Ravensbruck alive were as ravaged and critically ill as those who had survived there since the beginning of the war.

To Toto, Colonial Java, the madness and hedonism of Paris, the great and the good (and not so good) of Beaverbrook's London, and even the relative excitement of life on the run with the brave partisans of Italy seemed like a fantastical tale told by a stranger.

Years later, as an old woman, Toto finally and hesitantly recalled her first hours at Ravensbruck:

'It was a very cold day and I was utterly bewildered.

Remember, we knew nothing about the full extent of the concentration camps until either we entered one or until after Germany had been defeated. Until I got there, I thought it would be an extension of the prisons in Italy. On my first day there I saw a young woman, she must have been barely out her teens, suffering a miscarriage on the floor in the block I was taken to. She was removed to the camp hospital and I never saw her again.

Shortly afterwards I saw a group of prisoners pushing wheelbarrows containing dead bodies. I didn't realise it at the time – how could I – that this was the norm in this awful place. But what it did tell me was that if I was to survive I had to work out how to very quickly and not leave it to chance. But first I asked myself: Did I want to survive if this was the life I had to endure?'

Hitler, with the enthusiastic support of Himmler, had created his insane vision of a 'master race', free of Jews and free of the deaf, blind, mute, disabled and epileptic. All would be exterminated under the cover of war. So too would the gypsies, prostitutes, despised religious groups and spies – and all other 'worthless mouths' as Himmler liked to call them. These 'worthless' lives would simply be ended, according to Hitler's plan, removed by poison, or flames, or bullets and, in time, a new, pure Germany would be bred.

At Ravensbruck, it was obvious that the

commandant, Fritz Suhren, could neither cope with the number of prisoners nor the administrative structure needed to organise, control and exterminate them. Ordered destruction on a scale such as this is not that easy. Indeed, the number to be killed was of such magnitude that it would take time… And the longer it took, the greater the likelihood of internal insurrection or military defeat.

CHAPTER 19

CONTACTS IN HIGH PLACES

*'[Chanel] is a person who knows Churchill sufficiently
to undertake political negotiations with him.'*
– From a post-war note

The war was going badly for Germany. The invasion of
Russia had been a resounding humiliation for the Fuhrer;
the Allies' recapture of Italy was just a few months away;
and Berlin had been almost destroyed by Allied bombers.
Himmler, overseer of the Final Solution, realised that
the Fatherland could not win. With that weighing on his
mind, he had recruited a 33-year-old general, Walter
Schellenberg, his head of SS Intelligence, to see if the
neutral Swiss and Swedish might intermediate with the
British and negotiate an end to hostilities. Or as Himmler
himself put it: 'To find a way out of the raging sea of
blood of SS mass murders.' Extraordinary language
from the very architect of those mass murders…

Schellenberg was, as the American journalist
William L Shirer memorably called him, a 'university

educated intellectual gangster'. Or in the words of his post-war interrogators (including Helenus Milmo, whose withering verdict on Driberg's biography of Beaverbrook is noted earlier): 'A low character without standards of loyalty or common decency.' And, reportedly, a one-time lover of Chanel.

Dincklage too felt the world closing in on him, though life for the Nazi occupiers in Paris had changed little: Maxim's welcomed him and Coco, there was horse racing at Auteuil, and food and wine were still in plentiful supply – though only for the wealthy, connected elite. The rest of Paris starved. His sense of foreboding was ramped up somewhat when he was informed that de Gaulle and Free French had named him as a one of their 'most wanted', along with Chanel, and he had been advised to leave France for a safer country, possibly Turkey or Argentina. Chanel was distraught. She could not envisage life separated from her lover and, more importantly, her protector.

It was against this unstable background that the pair came up with an outrageous plan, one which might just save both of them from the fate they richly deserved. With the knowledge of Schellenberg, and maybe the blessing of Himmler, they would try to journey to Madrid again to meet Chanel's old friend Sir Samuel Hoare, the British ambassador to Spain. They convinced themselves that Hoare would then enlist her former lover, the Duke of Westminster, and 'Bendor' would then intercede with Churchill putting forward the case that there was sufficient support in Berlin to remove Hitler and reach a settlement with Britain.

Dincklage flew to Berlin in the hope of persuading his Abwehr superiors of Chanel's worth as an intermediary. Chanel waited, pacing and desperate for his return.

Back in Paris, he told Chanel of the devastation he had seen in Berlin. The war, he told her, was all but lost. Their mission was therefore of the most critical importance…not least if they were going to save their own skins. Westminster was, predictably, an enthusiastic supporter and pledged he would do his best to engage the prime minister on the matter.

The most senior Abwehr officers in Berlin vetoed the trip, however. And that, as far as they were concerned, was that. But the SS, in particular Schellenberg, had other ideas. What was known – by only a very select few – was that Himmler and others were looking for a way out of the war they had realised they would never win. Most notable among them was von Ribbentrop, once a friend of Beaverbrook and his daughter Janet, and who had entertained Toto at a weekend house party. So it came as a very pleasant shock to Dincklage when he received orders to bring Chanel to Berlin at once to plan the mission.

The journey itself would be wrought with danger. The flight from Le Bourget to Tempelhof airport was under threat of enemy fire, and the long rail trip could be bombed. But it had to be done, and the couple settled for the wagon-lit train from Paris's Gare du Nord to

Berlin's Zoologischer Garten station – risky, but relatively comfortable, with acceptable sleeping and dining facilities. They left the French capital just after 11pm, and arrived at 9.30pm the following evening, where they were met by Schellenberg's personally selected SS officers and two Mercedes. On the journey through and then out of Berlin, Chanel could see for herself, even in the darkness, just how devastated the city was. By contrast, Paris was mostly intact because of France's early capitulation.

Their destination was the SS guesthouse at Wannsee, a lake resort in the city's western district, complete with bombproof shelter…where much of the Holocaust had been planned.

The following morning the couple met with Schellenberg, and a post-war note of the meeting described Chanel as 'an enemy of Russia and desirous of helping France and Germany, whose destinies she believed to be closely linked.' It added: 'She is a person who knows Churchill sufficiently to undertake political negotiations with him.' Of course, if she had known him as well during the war as she had in the 1930s, she would have realised that Churchill was in no mood for talks other than for total German defeat: Unconditional Surrender. This had been agreed at a summit of the Allies earlier in the year in Casablanca, and there would no deviation from that.

At the meeting, Chanel made an unexpected demand. It involved Vera Bate Lombardi, her old friend and publicist (and distant relative of the royals and

Churchill), the English aristocrat who, despite being married to an Italian colonel and Fascist party member, had been interned as an 'alien' and held near Rome. Chanel, convinced that Bate, with her impeccable connections, would ensure the success of the mission, asked that she should be released to travel with her and Dincklage to Madrid. Seven days later, Bate *was* freed on the orders of Schellenberg and, as per the plan, she left with Chanel and Dincklage for Madrid, crossing the border at Hendaye where they were met by Dincklage's friend, one of the most odious SS men (even by their standards): Walter Kutschmann had been responsible for the massacre in 1942 of 1,500 intellectuals at Lwow, Poland, having first made the victims dig their own graves.

At the crossing, Kutschmann handed Dincklage a package for Chanel containing a very large, though unspecified, sum of money: Agent Westminster, the horizontal collaborator, was in Spain to bring peace…

When they arrived in Madrid, Chanel and Bate booked into the Ritz, and Dincklage headed for the German Embassy. Chanel was then taken to the British Embassy with a letter for Churchill and handed to a senior diplomat stationed there, Henry Hankey.

Chanel's handwritten six-page letter was sent to Downing Street; but the elaborately named 'Operation Modellhut', as her mission had been codenamed, now blew up in her horrified face.

In what she thought would be an unmitigated success, a done deal, there came a twist: Bate proceeded to denounce her friend Chanel as a German agent (which of course she was) to the British authorities. Not surprisingly, contact between the women ceased instantly.

The letter arrived at Number Ten when Churchill was away, as unbeknown to the newspapers, he was secretly in Tunisia, bedridden with pneumonia. Clementine read it instead. There was no direct reference to negotiating peace with Germany at all, but a self-serving ramble about how Chanel herself had intervened to have Vera Bate freed from prison, and could her husband somehow help to get her (Vera) out of Spain, where she was being held, and back to Italy. It began, 'My Dear Winston', and ended, 'I remain always affectionately.' What Clemmie actually thought of the strange letter will for ever be a mystery, but she no doubt read it with no little puzzlement.

On their return to Paris, Dincklage was told by Kutschmann to be prepared to flee to Argentina at a moment's notice, which is exactly what he did himself, having first gone to Vigo in Spain posing as a Carmelite monk. Fate finally caught up with this war criminal in 1975, but he escaped extradition from the country which had made itself a second home for Nazis.

For Chanel and Dincklage, it was time for Plan B. The trouble was, there was no Plan B...

CHAPTER 20

ONE LAST CARD TO PLAY

'In your camp, 2,000 people monthly have to die, Reichsfuhrer SS.'

– Himmler

Libraries are full of books on the Holocaust; and there are tens of thousands of pages of information and images online. Despite this, it is utterly impossible to understand how Hitler and his entourage bred so many unquestioning followers, millions of them, men and women, who either turned a blind eye or actually revelled in the unrelenting cruelty inflicted on their fellow man, who simply through birth were of another faith or culture, or born disabled in some way, or by choice followed a certain path or political persuasion.

Three days after Toto entered Ravensbruck, an order from Himmler was found on the commandant's desk by one of the prisoners assigned to work in the office: 'In your camp, 2,000 people monthly have to die, Reichsfuhrer SS.' Commandant Suhren proved up to the task, and the arrival of three specialists in mass murder would further speed the process.

Word spread around the camp. It was met with either absolute fear or exhausted resignation.

But it was the arrival of Carl Clauberg that caused the greatest terror. He specialised in sterilisation surgery, 'justified' after the passing in 1933 of the sinister-sounding Law for the Prevention of Genetically Defective Progeny, one of Hitler's most odious pieces of Nazi legislation. Clauberg's task was to find a way to implement the wholesale sterilising of fertile women as quickly and as effortlessly as possible, and of what consequence was the pain and after effects? Jews, gypsies, the blind and deaf; in short, anybody who did not fit the perfect Aryan model. As for Toto, a bisexual mixed race woman and Resistance fighter…would she escape the brutality of enforced sterilisation?

The sterilisation programme was put in motion, much to Clauberg's depraved pleasure. Fallopian tubes were blocked by intravenous injections containing a mixture of iodine and silver nitrate using unsterilised needles. It worked, but at appalling cost to the women who suffered from vaginal and internal bleeding, excruciating pain, and in many cases cervical cancer. Refusal to take part was met with execution – a welcome alternative.

The weeks passed and Toto, by then a prisoner for more than two months, was in an appalling state from the hard manual work, lack of sleep and severe malnourishment. She weighed little more than five stones (70 pounds/32 kilograms), and was in an intense state of mental and physical breakdown.

She was not alone, of course. Every woman in the camp was suffering from the relentless hours spent in the freezing cold unloading sand from lorries and mixing it with cement 'to repair roads'. But it was a case of work for work's sake, as there were few potholes to be mended.

On other days, they were ordered to mix their own excrement with the still-warm ashes and crushed bones of bodies from the crematorium – the Nazi version of fertiliser for the vegetable plots. These supposed vegetables were never seen. They certainly weren't fed to the women forced to survive on the mouldy bread that had been saved for them, and the foul liquid they were told was 'soup'.

The scenes every day were unimaginable. Women who arrived pregnant often miscarried, and their aborted foetuses lay where they were expelled in the vomit and excrement; those who gave birth could not feed their new-born, so it would die mewling with the pain of starvation; one young mother saw her baby eaten by rats; those returning from being sterilised screamed in agony, bleeding and hoping for death.

Toto decided to play the last card she had, one that might save her life, for her last ounces of strength were waning shovelling sand and bones in the cold: she went to see the camp doctor, a man called Karl Gebhardt, whose credentials were highlighted by failure to assist a single human soul. He even failed to save the life of

Reinhard Heydrich, another of the principal architects of the Holocaust. Heydrich had been wounded by an anti-tank grenade thrown by a brave Czech Resistance fighter trained in England. Following surgery, he had developed a fever, and Gebhardt was told by Hitler's own doctor to treat the patient with an early antibiotic called sulphonamide. He disobeyed the instruction, and Heydrich died. Thereafter, he became obsessed with experimenting with the drug, and the prisoners at Ravensbruck provided him with a ceaseless supply of human guinea pigs.

Toto told Gebhardt she was a fully qualified nurse, trained at St Mary's Hospital, London.[33] She knew there would be no checks. A Nazi death camp could hardly write to a London hospital asking for references for a job applicant. It was typical of her crazy ingenuity, but the stakes were now dangerously high: failure to secure work in the hospital would almost certainly mean her death.

She was immediately recruited and sent to work in Block 6, better known as the 'Death Quarters'. Other than the 'nurses' who were prisoners, the staff mainly consisted of German soldiers, many of whom delighted in the pain they inflicted. And nobody more so than Gebhardt's assistant, Dr Herta Oberheuser, a 33-year-old dermatologist and dedicated Nazi who had arrived at Ravensbruck in 1942, ready and willing to do her worst. Part of that willingness involved carrying out appalling

---

[33] The nearest she had come to nursing were the rudimentary first aid lessons at school in Holland, and at her finishing school in London.

experiments on women who had bones removed without anaesthesia, which were then transplanted into other women, also without anaesthesia. The pain and trauma to these women was unimaginable, begging, once more, the question: How did Hitler and his entourage breed so many unquestioning followers, willing to carry out such monstrous orders on their fellow man? And what of the women happy to inflict such suffering on their own kind? Men, we know too well, are capable of all manner of horrific behaviours, but women? The apparent reason for these barbaric acts was to further the Nazi's knowledge in treating battle-wounded German soldiers.

Though it involved no real physical labour, the psychological toll of work in the 'hospital' on Toto was horrific. In the case of injury, or the results of being badly whipped or beaten, there was little or no basic medical equipment, no bandages, nothing was sterile, and there was no pain relief, not to mention the deliberate lack of anaesthesia. The place was filthy, and most 'patients' ended up in the crematorium. Many who were admitted with cholera or typhus would never recover either.

Toto did her best to help the patients in any way she could. She would bring food and give it to the more able bodied, those who stood a chance of living – if they wanted to live, that was. She hid women destined for the gas chambers in the hospital's lavatory block. She falsified medical charts, anything that might delay the SS in sending a woman to her death.

In an attempt to bring even a moment of distraction

to these broken women she organised an impromptu fashion show, with the women modelling various ways of wearing the striped rags they barely stood up in. Most of all, she spent time talking to them, trying to cheer them by telling them about her time in Paris and London, and her life with the Resistance in Italy. Unlike some storytellers, she had no need to exaggerate. There is little doubt that she saved some lives and, quite possibly, a little sanity too.

Toto spent just four months in the hospital, using her failing strength and determination to achieve a little good in circumstances beyond her darkest imaginings. But then came the final blow: Oberheuser sent for her. She was to be sterilised.

She had done everything to bring some humanity to her inhumane surroundings, but she now knew, for the first time in her life that she was giving up.

*

When Hitler took over as chancellor in 1933 the country was in dire straits following its humiliation at the Treaty of Versailles. He quickly eliminated unemployment, concentrating on a massive re-armament programme. By the time war came, Germany was strong once again and, for some of his wicked faithful – the likes of Carl Clauberg, Otto Moll, Rudolf Hoss and Albert Sauer, to name but a few, and all of whom had fled the march of the Red Army – places like Ravensbruck and Auschwitz became their new ghastly playgrounds.

Himmler often visited his 'masterpiece', Ravensbruck, and one trip coincided with a protest by a group of Jehovah's Witnesses who refused to sew mailbags or work outside in the freezing winter conditions. (Their religion forbade that followers take part in anything that constituted 'war work'.) As punishment these women were first forced to stand in their flimsy shift dresses for hours in the snow until, one by one, they collapsed. Then they were locked in unheated stone cells, nine to each cell, in total darkness with no food. On the day Himmler visited, they had been there for three weeks, and not one of them had broken their resolve. The Reichsfuhrer went to see these brave women and was unmoved. Incredibly, they survived and spent the rest of their days at Ravensbruck working as cleaners in the homes of SS guards.

Aside from Toto's efforts, there were countless acts of bravery – or madness, perhaps – at Ravensbruck. Towards the end of the war, when some prisoners were being selected for release, 400 French women were lined up outside. Half of them were told they would be freed. When they were dismissed, three were told to stay behind, all of them aristocrats: Christiane de Cuerville, Colette de Dumast and Jacqueline d'Alincourt. Each was given a piece of paper and were told they would be released if they wrote that they had been treated well at the camp. Their reply was a resounding Non! All three were brutally punished.

But for Toto, she had played her last card. No

punishment or threat or order remained that could shock her. Devoid now of all hope, she prepared to die.

CHAPTER 21

THE HORIZONTAL GAMBLER

*'Paris! Paris ravaged! Paris broken! Paris martyred!
But Paris free!'*
— General Charles de Gaulle

By the middle of 1944 the Allies had landed in Normandy and were on their way to Paris. In July of the same year, Hitler survived the von Stauffenberg assassination attempt, Operation Valkyrie, but the game was up for him and his malevolent band of cheerleaders.

Chanel was now in absolutely no doubt that Germany was about to lose the war, and feared she would end up branded as a collaborator — or as the Free French dubbed her: a 'horizontal collaborator' — and her head would be shaved, her chest branded with a swastika, and she would be paraded through the streets of Paris like so many of her fellow horizontals.

Black smoke filtered up through chimneys into the skies over Paris as Dincklage and his fellow SS and Gestapo officers frantically burned incriminating papers in preparation for the liberation of the capital. Allied bombs were falling on the outskirts of Paris, and all eyes were on the flag poles and lamp posts of the city to see if the swastika flags had been taken down. The Ritz emptied rapidly of its senior Nazi guests. Dincklage fled the inevitable and made for Germany.

Chanel, alone except for her faithful maid and butler, moved to her apartment in Rue Cambon and contacted her old on-off lover Pierre Reverdy, a French Resistance fighter. Desperate, she urged him to find and arrest Baron Louis de Vaufreland, her one-time fellow traveller on her first mission to Madrid. She knew he would be the first to implicate her as Agent Westminster and must be silenced. She didn't care how. She had money – much of it accumulated from the Nazi elite buying her perfume with the gold seized from France's Jewish population – and would do anything and pay whatever was necessary to save her own skin.

Her plan – if such an ill-thought-out order born of desperation could be called such – worked. Vaufreland was found hiding in a friend's apartment and was arrested and thrown into jail. But if she had taken the time to think the thing through properly, she would have realised that, under questioning, Vaufreland wouldn't hesitate to reveal the extent of her activities, which amounted to much more than simply sleeping with the enemy.

How could she make sure he would not talk?

On 25th August, a stiflingly hot day, General Charles

de Gaulle entered a newly liberated Paris; the following day, just as Hitler had done four years earlier, he marched down the Champs-Élysée to Notre Dame and proclaimed: *'Paris! Paris ravaged! Paris broken! Paris martyred! But Paris free!'*

Chanel watched the ecstatic, triumphant man's parade from the balcony of Josep Maria Sert's apartment. The following nights passed without sleep as she waited, in cold fear, for the hammering on the door.

Two weeks later it came. She had gambled once too often. Chanel was arrested.

CHAPTER 22

THE FINAL ORDER

"Meine damen, sie sind frei." ("Ladies, you are free.")

       – German commander, Fritz Suhren

Scraps of news were whispered to old prisoners from new – about Paris, about Germany, about swastikas being burned and declarations of victory – but for the women dehumanised by incarceration at Ravensbruck, it meant little. Barely alive, they heard the words but stared through eyes so accustomed to horror that hope simply failed to stir.

Senior Nazis, terrified for their own lives now, had turned against Hitler – most notably Himmler, who was sufficiently deranged to think he could broker a peaceful settlement with the Allies and take over from Hitler.

As part of his plan, he authorised General Walter Schellenberg, by then SS Intelligence chief, to begin negotiations with the International Red Cross to allow the release of prisoners. As a consequence, Count Folke

Bernadotte, of the Swedish Red Cross, flew to Berlin to visit Schellenberg and Himmler to ask for the release of the Scandinavians held at Ravensbruck. In a subsequent meeting, however, the count asked that the release be extended to others, and on 9th April 1945 he was given permission to contact Ravensbruck's commandant, Fritz Suhren, and arrange for the transfer of the emaciated, diseased and dying women to his care.

Eight days later, a convoy of buses, trucks, ambulances and motorcycles, manned by Swedish doctors and nurses, arrived, the tops and sides of the vehicles emblazoned with large red crosses to ensure Allied planes would not attack. They had little time to spare. The daily killings were at their peak, and the crematorium was running 24 hours a day, every day. People in neighbouring villages had started complaining about the nauseating smell, the constant black smoke, and the ash which fell in thick layers in the fields and on the houses. One prisoner managed to get a letter out to Norwegian friends: *'Thousands have been picked out and sent to the gas chamber. A number of them were ill, but some were quite well, though older.'*

Himmler argued that his co-operation with the release of prisoners had to be repaid by Bernadotte, putting his own name forward as an intermediary with the Allies, which would lead to the removal of Hitler and the installation of Himmler himself. He even tried to convince Bernadotte that he was anxious to liberate the Jewish prisoners in his desperation to prove to the world that the Fuhrer, and he alone, was responsible for the grim catalogue of barbarity; that he, the decent, reasonable Himmler, was a man they could do business with. It was pure fantasy, and the count did absolutely nothing of the sort. The architect of the Holocaust was left to face the inevitable consequences of his sickening behaviour.

Two days before the Swedish convoy arrived, the Bergen-Belsen camp had been reached and liberated by the British. Many of the Ravensbruck women had been transferred to Belsen, and as one British medical officer reported: 'The unclothed bodies of women in a pile 60 to 80 yards long, 30 yards wide and four feet high, within sight of children. Gutters were filled with dead. Men had gone to gutters to die. Thousands were dying of typhus, TB and dysentery. There was no flesh on the bodies but the liver, kidneys and heart were cut out.' It seemed the horrors of Ravensbruck had been surpassed, if such were even possible.

On 23rd April, Toto and some of the women laid around her were ordered to 'get into the showers'. Toto knew her time had come, as these were the words that had first been used to take women to the gas chambers. But, as she slowly raised her eyes, she realised they had been taken to the shower block, where they were handed new clothes. They were told they were to be freed.

Toto's friend, a fellow Dutch woman called Jeanne Bommejin de Rochement, wrote: 'We leave the camp… moving in the direction of the gas chambers, and for many of us this is too much. A few are seized by a kind of nervous fit and we have to calm them…then we see men who do not beat us, shout and swear at us…there are tears in their eyes when they see us. Then we are off, stared at by the SS and the guards whom we mock to their faces. We can mock at them now.' And later: 'This sounds too good to be true and we do not believe it, we know better.'

The women had not slept for more than 24 hours and had spent most of the night outside their block talking. Jeanne wrote: 'We are nervous, very nervous, even if we pretend we are not. Like two children we play our little game of make-believe, what it will be like to be home again, who will be there to receive us, where shall we go. Then we go back in the hut which is dreadful, the smell overpowering.'

They were made to wait until 5pm that afternoon, after a lunch of turnip soup and bread; and then Toto and the bedraggled, skeletal group of women, once full of life, fun and love, emerged from the squalid hell of Ravensbruck clutching another piece of bread all released prisoners had been given. Barely able to walk, she boarded one of 12 white coaches. For the ongoing journey, the convoy had brought along a truck full of water, and basic food…the sort that women who have been starved for months and even years would be able to digest.

Nelly Langholm, a Norwegian woman who was with Toto, later wrote: 'We came out in our new clothes and had to walk to the gate. We saw the buses, and there were

Swedish men in grey uniforms with red crosses on their arms. They were just standing outside the gate. I think they told us: "Now you will go to Sweden…now you will be free." Before we left, the German big boss[34] came out and said: "Meine damen, sie sind frei." ("Ladies, you are free.") Can you imagine? Here was a German calling us Meine Damen. Were they really talking to us? We hadn't been called ladies for such a long time. Mein damen…'

It was four days after Hitler's 56th and final birthday, and they were on their way. In the distance was the sound of the Red Army's firepower.

During the 500-mile coach and ferry marathon to Sweden, doctors checked on the women and treated them as best they could, but sadly, not all them survived the week-long journey which was hazardous in the extreme. Not only were the roads in an appalling state, but the women were too, and some simply didn't have the strength to stay alive. There were frequent stops at check points, and so the women could relieve themselves in the fields, and Allied air raids had to be dodged. As Toto told Laura Aitken: *'After all we had gone through, we were bombed by our own side for much of the way.'*

One woman said later: 'When we saw the grass, the green grass…we hadn't seen green grass for two years. So Margarethe and I asked if we could get down from the bus and go into the grass. We wanted to pee in the grass. So they let us down and we ran across the field and

---

[34] Suhren, presumably.

took our knickers down. I will never forget the feeling of the green grass. It was a feeling so beautiful, cool and soft. Freedom, you know…'

Toto was unrecognisable from the beautiful young thing that dazzled Paris and London. She had lost almost half her body weight, and her hair was a rough stubble. Her face was lined and grey; her eyes no longer sparkled. She was a shrunken, hunched creature.

But she had survived.

PART THREE

IT WAS THE SPRING OF HOPE

CHAPTER 23

LIES AND TRUTH

'Churchill had me freed…'

— Coco Chanel

German soldiers who failed to escape Paris in time were rounded up and thrown into camps and prisons – by all accounts, 12,000 of them – and their French counterparts faced trial by special courts the following month. If found guilty, they would either be imprisoned or executed. Some would be spared, but would never be able to practice in the professions again or vote.

As for Chanel, she had been on the Free French blacklist since 1942, and in September 1944 she had been taken to their offices for questioning. Extraordinarily, her interrogators seemed to know nothing about her role as a Nazi agent or of her work with and for the Abwehr. And, crucially, they were ignorant of Modellhut, her half-baked and self-serving mission to Madrid posing as a go-between in the hope of getting Churchill to seek peace with Hitler. The Free French had failed to do any basic homework on the woman and, as a result, Chanel was back at her apartment in Rue Cambon that same day.

She told her maid Germaine: *'Churchill had me freed.'* But what was the truth?

In the late 1920s and through the '30s, she and Churchill were on good terms. Certainly, he was one of her admirers, as we recall from his letter to Clemmie stating, *'The famous Chanel turned up and I took a great fancy to her – a most capable woman…'* They'd dined together at the Ritz and corresponded, before he'd joined the Cabinet. But in 1944, as the tide of war had turned in the favour of the Allies, would the prime minister really have had either the time or inclination to rescue a woman he would have known was a Nazi agent? Some claim that Churchill instructed Duff Cooper, his ambassador to the Free French, to intervene. The argument is also put forward that Churchill could not have risked her being put on trial, because she knew too much about the Nazi sympathies of the Duke and Duchess of Windsor, and that the wartime prime minister had contravened his own government's Trading with the Enemy Act by paying the Germans to protect the Windsor's Paris apartment while they were safely away in the Bahamas. Those bloody Windsors; still a problem even as victory was within his grasp…

In a blatant attempt to show she was much relieved that the Allies were the winning side, Chanel pulled what she must have regarded as her get-out-of-jail card. Malcolm Muggeridge, the journalist, polemicist and, at that time, an MI6 officer in Paris, marvelled at the way she had escaped what seemed her inevitable fate in France: 'By one of those majestically simple strokes which made Napoleon so successful a general, she just put an announcement in the window of her emporium that her perfume was available free to GIs.' Many things she may have been, but her instinct for self-preservation was always top of the list.

Then came an urgent message from 'Bendor' Westminster: *'Don't lose a minute. Get out of France.'* Was he just the messenger, with the advice coming from elsewhere? Or was he using his judgement, reckoning that de Gaulle would be bound on revenge?

Three hours later, Chanel left Rue Cambon, her Cadillac piled high with cases, and headed for Lausanne in neutral Switzerland. That in itself is revealing. Paris was empty of cars. The fleeing Germans had escaped in theirs, and the only vehicles were for use by the Allied liberators. What's more, somehow she had got hold of enough petrol for the trip. Was this a case of having money enough to buy her way out of trouble? Or was it because she conveniently knew the right people? If she did, who were those people?

Chanel arrived in Lausanne and settled at the Beau Rivage hotel on Lake Leman, where she stayed until she bought a house nearby. Her old friend, Misia Sert was a regular visitor. Bound by their severe morphine addiction, and to service the habit, they made immediately for a pharmacy in Lausanne, where they established a 'favourable relationship' with the pharmacist. Their habit was engrained, and prolific, and Sert made no attempt to hide injecting herself in full view while out shopping. And there was no shortage of money to fund the habit, in fact to fund any of their vices: on his earlier visits to Switzerland Dincklage had deposited enormous quantities of gold in the country's secretive banks. Strangely, however, there was no sign of him, and Chanel was fretting. Where was he? Was he was being hidden by friends in Germany or Austria? Or had he been captured? But she also had other things on her mind and, if she was honest, Dincklage was the least of her worries.

In fact, Dincklage had left his hiding place and was on his way to the family estate, Rosencrantz Manor near Schinkel in northern Germany, where his mother had spent the war. He was with a friend, Hans Schillinger, when they were stopped by a British patrol. A search revealed that Dincklage was carrying money far in excess of the permitted amount: $8,000, 1,340 Norwegian kroner, 100 Slovak koruna and 33 gold pieces. They were immediately arrested and, when questioned, Schillinger said he had collected the currencies in Paris from Chanel Parfums to be given to Dincklage. The money was confiscated, but once again few awkward questions were asked, despite the fact that they had seriously violated regulations.

Back in Paris, her accusers had not given up, and in May 1946 the case against her came before the Cour de Justice…and the presiding judge, Roger Serre, had before him documents showing her role as agent F-7124, Agent Westminster. They also had letters and reports for the Abwehr, written by Vaufreland, who was being investigated separately. She was in great danger, and it was unlikely to go away, but she did not travel there to answer the charges and remained resolutely in Lausanne.

Three years later, Chanel could hold out no further and had to return to Paris to face charges before Judge Fernand Paul Leclercq. A summary of proceedings should read: '*The accused denied everything and lied her head off.*'

On Vaufreland, she claimed: 'It was completely by accident that we met on the train. I was happy to find myself with him in Madrid because he spoke the language fluently.' She also provided him a free character assassination: 'A frivolous young man speaking a lot of nonsense […] visibly of abnormal morals[35], and everything in his manner of dressing and perfuming himself revealed what he was. I didn't trust him […] if he was in relations with certain Germans it could only be of a sexual nature.'

Of the release of her nephew Andre from a PoW camp: 'I cannot say if this was due or not to the intervention of the Germans at the request of Vaufreland.'

On her lover: 'The only German I knew during the occupation was the Baron Dincklage, established in France before the war and married to an Israelite.'

---

[35] This from an anti-Semitic, promiscuously bisexual drug addict!

When advised of testimony from Vaufreland that he had helped Chanel get in touch with the Nazi authorities running the Aryanisation of properties programme in order to wrest ownership back from the Wertheimers she said: 'The Chanel establishments were never sequestered. There was a temporary administration for around three weeks and the businesses Aryanised thanks to a scheme of the Wertheimers.'

And referring to her first visit to Spain, she claimed she was there to secure material needed for the manufacture of her perfumes and said: 'While at the British Embassy I wanted above all to have news of the Duke of Westminster, who was very ill at the time.'

Strangely, the court never questioned her about the second trip to Madrid, or about the nature of her relationship with Dincklage. But it did put to her the Abwehr records, that she had been registered as an agent. Her response: 'I was never aware of my registration in a German service and I protest with indignation against such an absurdity.'

All this, we understand, she declared with a straight face. Though it is not recorded if her nose grew longer during testimony…

To recall what Toto had said about Chanel many years before: '…*she was too concerned with her own wealth to worry about what was right and wrong.*'

But, as Vera Bate had done in Madrid, Chanel's nephew Andre Palasse, the PoW released through the intervention of her Nazi friends, told the truth. 'I didn't know Vaufreland before the war […] Mademoiselle Chanel told me she had asked Vaufreland to use all his influence to get me freed. I have no proof of it […] I repeat, I only knew what Mademoiselle Chanel told me.'

On 13th July 1949, Vaufreland was found guilty of co-operating with the enemy and sentenced to six years imprisonment.

As for his very own Judas, Chanel, she returned to Lausanne, but with a shadow, dark and persistent, hanging over her.

In another trial, Otto Abetz, the chief Nazi representative in Paris who had hosted Chanel at lavish dinner parties, at which she spewed her anti-Semitic views, was given 20 years hard labour.

Judge Leclercq noted: 'The answers Mademoiselle Chanel gave were deceptive. The court will decide if the case should be pursued.'

But the case against Chanel was never pursued, and there was little media reporting of her court case, which was all very odd. Chanel was as high profile a figure as could be imagined; an international and fabulously rich designer and parfumier. Yet only the briefest coverage in the newspapers in France and elsewhere resulted. Of course there were bigger fish than Chanel who needed to be dealt with; but there were few more famous than the almost-disgraced Chanel – and as we know, the media, then as now, likes nothing more than a famous falling from grace.

Maybe it was all down to a general exhaustion with the war, and a universal wish to lay the whole sordid thing to rest. But if that was the case, why were so many others brought to justice and punished?

Why also was the full extent of Chanel's activities – not just the collaboration, but her role as Agent Westminster – kept secret for almost 40 years? The files were locked away in the archives of the French, German, Italian, US and Soviet governments, and it was not until 1985 that, following agreement between Moscow and Paris, the files were sent to the French military archive at Chateau de Vincennes.

Not only that, within two months Dincklage joined his lover in Lausanne, one of the very few senior Nazis to go unpunished. It seems that Chanel, and maybe by association Dincklage, had been placed above the law. But by whom?

CHAPTER 24

ONIONS, GARLIC AND A WIG

'She was no longer the woman I knew in Italy.'
– The journalist, William Rospigliosi

Toto was taken to Gothenburg, Sweden's second city. All of the hotels and hostels were full, having been offered to returning soldiers. The Red Cross managed to get some of the women into the last remaining rooms, but not Toto and her companions. Instead they were taken to the city's Natural History Museum, where 80 other Ravensbruck women were being nursed. Toto was in a pitiful state. She now weighed less than five stones, her skin was translucent, her muscles wasted. Severely malnourished and weak, she could barely eat, and struggled to swallow even the smallest mouthfuls of food.

Her friend, the journalist William Rospigliosi, said, 'Mistreatment and malnutrition had caused pulmonary weakness. And sadly the mutilations she underwent when being sterilised – in the most filthy conditions, remember – left her scarred in both mind and body […]

This was no longer the Toto I knew in Italy. She was aggressive, something I had never seen with her before, and psychologically very damaged.' Elizabeth Eichmann agreed: 'Her time with the Resistance and the periods in jail had taken their toll but much less than might be expected. But seven months in Ravensbruck almost destroyed her.'

Learning of her release, her former lover, Randolph Churchill, knew what Toto needed: onions and garlic, which act as a blood cleanser, reduce bad bacteria and are a natural antibiotic. Through the Red Cross he sent vast quantities of these, which Toto shared with the women around her.

She then received another parcel from Randolph. It contained a wig, and some lipstick. We can only imagine the smile, maybe even the tears that accompanied this thoughtful gift.

The second week Toto was in the museum, Randolph Churchill arrived in person, not with garlic, but with money, clothes and another wig. He had been given permission to travel from Yugoslavia, where he was part of Fitzroy Maclean's military and diplomatic mission. He was shocked to see how frail and emaciated his once vibrant and beautiful lover was, and the clothes he'd brought had to be safety pinned to fit. But they were able to go for a short walk in the spring sunshine, and Toto even gave Randolph a short conducted tour of the museum, particularly the dinosaur in the palaeontology gallery. Her bed was positioned right next to it.

Randolph brought news of Max and his father. Max had distinguished himself during the war and was now a much decorated Group Captain with awards of the Distinguished Service Order, Distinguished Flying Cross and the Czechoslovakian War Cross. He was yet to remarry. Of his father, Toto learned that he had been one of the originators of the Allied victory by ensuring that, under his eccentric and determined authority, Britain had enough fighter planes to win the Battle of Britain. Without those planes, who knows what might have been the fate of the country, and even the world? He sent his good wishes to Toto, the woman he had once hurled abuse at, calling her a 'bloody negress' and a 'whore', and arranged for money to be sent to her.

Her brother Ody visited her too, shocked to see his sister in such a weakened state, and horrified by the recounting of her last seven months. He spent much of his stay with her reminiscing about their parents and their idyllic childhood in Java. But those memories seemed to cause Toto great distress.

Like the other evacuees, Toto also received money from the Red Cross, and she knew she must somehow start planning a future and find somewhere sunny to recuperate.

When she was slightly stronger, Randolph took her to Stockholm. She wrote to Elizabeth Eichmann: '*I was lucky that Randolph came here, and as I am an old love of his he made a terrible fuss of me and took me all over to Stockholm for the papers.*' She was referring to a passport, and other documents that would enable her to eventually leave Sweden.

Ody tried to persuade her to return with him to Holland, but Toto, a glimmer of her former independence emerging, had another plan. She wanted go to Switzerland.

Would she have gone, we might ask, if she had known Switzerland was home to one self-indulgent, anti-Semitic, self-obsessed Coco Chanel?

CHAPTER 25

THE PAPERS, LETTER WRITING AND REST

'Boredom was just what I needed.'

– Toto

Toto travelled to Ascona, a small medieval town on the edge of Lake Maggiore in Switzerland. It had been untroubled by the war which had taken such a terrible toll on the rest of Europe, and was exactly what she needed. Peaceful, with a temperate climate, she was able to take slow walks around the lake or in the gentle hills and enjoy the pure, clean, restorative air. She knew this was exactly what was required to heal; but also knew it would not happen overnight. It would be a disciplined but traumatic journey back to some semblance of life.

There were barely 3,000 other inhabitants in Ascona, and most lived by Switzerland's famous reputation for quiet and privacy – indeed, many chose to live there because of it. But they were also there – a mixture of most European nationalities – because of country's neutrality during the war.

Money was not a problem for Toto, thanks to back payments from Lord Beaverbrook, and she had the best part of £500,000 (in today's values) in the bank, opened on her behalf by Randolph Churchill. The Beaver, despite or maybe because of his fortune, had a reputation for being difficult where money was concerned. But with Toto there were no quibbles, no questions. They were friends again, and he was open in his admiration for what she had tried to do for the Allied cause.

The first two weeks were spent in the Hotel Ascovilla, where she slept for hours upon hours and ate simply: eggs, vegetables and fruit. She registered with a local doctor who, to her surprise and relief, found her to be reasonably fit physically. The internal injuries caused by the sterilisation at Ravensbruck were healing, and the pain and bleeding had stopped. She was also gaining a little weight.

Toto then moved into a small house, rented from banker and art collector, Baron Eduard von der Heydt. The baron was German, and had been a member of the Nazi party, but left for Switzerland in 1939, relinquishing his membership and becoming a Swiss citizen.

She spent much time writing to friends, in between the walking and resting, and catching up with her greatest love, Max Aitken, who, she was amazed to hear, was now a Conservative MP for the London constituency of Holborn and a director of Express Newspapers. It was Max who told her that another former lover, Valentine Castlerosse, had died of a heart attack in 1943 at the age of 51, which saddened her. Her longest letters were to her closest platonic girlfriend Elizabeth Eichmann, still in Italy and by then translating for the British forces. Elizabeth wrote long letters in return, the exchange boosting both of their morales.

But nightmares and flashbacks were a frequent night-time companion, as is the case with so many victims of terrible trauma, and almost always appear only when a person has reached safety. When Toto woke after a nightmare she would immediately do some simple exercises – press-ups, sit-ups, running on the spot, anything. She said: '*It was the way I cleared my head of awful images which came back with great regularity. Gradually they went for good. Fortunately I had never experienced depression in my life, that was a godsend.*'

The routine of walking, letter writing, resting, enjoying the occasional swim, reading the English and French newspapers – which arrived four or five days after their date of publication – and cooking simple meals for herself was deeply calming. She even hired a rowing boat, and meandered around the lake, watching with fascination the array of wildfowl. She said, '*I was bored for the first time in my life and, after the madness of what I had experienced, boredom was just what I needed. I loved it, I really did!*'

But a woman like Toto, vibrant and adventurous by nature, could only take so much of the peace and quiet of Ascona and, after 15 months of blissful boredom, her world shifted once more. She met Erica Brausen.

CHAPTER 26

THE COST OF EXILE

'She didn't look like the Coco I knew.'

— The photographer, Horst

As we know, nearly 300 miles to the west of Switzerland, Coco Chanel, richer by far than her fellow citizens, was living in great luxury, first in the uber-chic Beau Rivage hotel on the shores of Lake Geneva, and then in a house in the hills at Lac de Saubablin.[36] She was heard to say, 'I couldn't live on the lake, which is hideous, with swans that smell,' adding, 'The house was small, my little suburban villa…' How the recovering French, doing their best to put the years of occupation behind them, must have balked at her open vulgarity.

She couldn't rewind and delete her history, however, and lived in constant dread that her former Nazi friends, those who had escaped execution, might one day name and shame her. Dincklage had now joined her — like his

---

[36] Which David Bowie bought after her death.

lover, having also escaped punishment – and the couple spent their days doing little, occasionally lunching out with the few friends who came to see them. But why had they escaped? And how? Who had intervened to save the pair? Could it really have been Churchill? Sticking to her 'truth', Chanel made sure that was the story in circulation.

When she wasn't obsessing over her two overriding preoccupations – increasing her wealth and securing the continued silence of her former Nazi friends, Chanel would be seen sitting in the lobby scowling at passers-by. As one observer said: 'When she was sitting in the lobby of the Beau Rivage she had the eyes of an eagle, she didn't miss anything. She didn't like the way the women dressed, whether they were foreigners or the wives of doctors and industrialists. "They lack class," she said.' The great couturier was hankering after her former life as the world's best known and most acclaimed designer, and unashamedly vociferous about it.

Still bitter and twisted about her perfume deal with her despised Jews, she heard that Pierre Wertheimer had discovered that (in breach of their 1924 agreement) she had still been making perfumes. He immediately left New York for Paris, and went straight for her lawyer Rene de Chambrun in the Champs-Élysées, not to injunct her but to do another deal. What he didn't know was that Chanel knew he knew, and had surreptitiously journeyed from Switzerland to be in the next room – obviously without his knowledge – for a consultation with her lawyer. By the end of the day she would be wealthier still: an immediate payment of £3 million, plus two per cent of all annual sales, the equivalent of £20 million a year (in today's values) were wired to her account. As she herself said: '*Now* I'm rich.'

There was yet another bug to deal with: Himmler's right-hand man, General Walter Schellenberg, her old friend and, it was rumoured, another of her lovers, and the man who had given the go-ahead for Operation Modellhut. He had been sentenced to six years for war crimes at the Nuremberg Trials – lenient because he testified against others in the SS – but had served just two years having been released on the grounds of ill health. He had not been idle in prison, however…and had written his memoirs, *The Labyrinth,* which was not good news for the exile in Lausanne. Chanel knew the past had to buried, and deeply, if there was to be any chance of a comeback to dominate couture once more, so she threw money at the problem, first by financing a house in Switzerland for Schellenberg and his wife Irene, and then by paying his medical bills for the treatment of his terminal liver cancer.

But this was far from straightforward. The Swiss authorities had no intention of allowing a Nazi war criminal to stay in their country so, on top of the medical bills she settled, totalling at least £100,000 (in today's values), she paid for another house for them, a villa at Pallanza, Italy, on the shores of Lake Maggiore…and just over the border from Toto. There he spent the rest of his days, living under the name of Louis Kowalki and carrying a forged Swiss passport. Before he died, Chanel made sure she received his absolute assurance that she would not appear in the pages of *The Labyrinth*.

The Swiss were inconsistent about Nazi criminals, however, because they did not object to Dincklage staying with Chanel at Lausanne, presumably because, mysteriously, he had never been convicted of a war crime, and neither had she. So the couple continued a life of idleness, occasionally receiving visitors, having lunch with friends, or venturing to Italy for holidays. When they met friends for lunch, Chanel's choice was always the same: vegetable soup, filet mignon, unbuttered rice and fruit compote. And morphine.

One visit was by the great photographer Horst Bohrmann in 1951. He reported: 'Chanel was somewhat lost at that time in her life; she seemed bored. Her hair was different and she had started to pluck her eyebrows. She didn't look like the Chanel I had known.'

In Rue Cambon, in post-war Paris, the Chanel boutique lay empty, mannequins unclothed. The cutting room remained eerily silent and, three floors above, her apartment gathered dust.

Had she abandoned all thoughts of returning? Would she even be able to?

CHAPTER 27

A CHANCE MEETING

'It was as if my old nanny Djim had come back to look after me'

– Toto

On a crisp November morning in 1946 Toto went to the post office in Ascona to send letters to Lord Beaverbrook at Cherkley and to Ody in Amsterdam. She decided to stop for coffee in the little café attached to the post office and there, at the next table, was a woman speaking brusquely in guttural German. Toto watched her for a while.

Erica Brausen was a 38-year-old German, just nine months older than Toto, but who looked nine years her senior. She had none of the beauty which Toto was slowly regaining, and had what used to be known as a 'matronly' figure. Though she seemed brusque, there was a great warmth about her…and Toto introduced herself.

Erica was from a well-off middle-class family in Dusseldorf, and though not Jewish they'd feared what was in store for liberals like them under Hitler and the

Nazis. Erica had been the first of the Brausens to leave Dusseldorf when she left for Paris in 1932, sharing a house in Montparnasse with the arty crowd. In 1935 she relocated to Majorca, at the invitation of her greatest male friend Joan Miro, the Spanish painter and sculptor. And there her life had begun to mirror Toto's.

She'd run a bar on the island frequented by artists and writers – at least that was her cover. Erica, in fact, under the unlikely codename Beryl, was liaising with the visiting US Navy to smuggle her Jewish and socialist friends out from under the grip of Franco's regime during the Spanish Civil War. Eventually she decided to leave herself, fearing what would happen if she was caught by the Fascist authorities. She arrived in London aboard a Spanish fishing boat, penniless, and with world war about to break out. But England's capital was not the easiest destination for an artistic 31-year-old German woman with no money and no friends.

In 1940 she married an artist, but it was far from a traditional union: Erica was a lesbian and her husband was homosexual. Their sexual preferences were irrelevant, however, as, more importantly, he was English and that meant that his unlikely bride could stay in the country legally. She had spent the war years trying to bring a little light relief to the capital by organising exhibitions in artists' studios and then working for a small but established gallery, the Redfern in Mayfair. Just before heading to Switzerland, and meeting Toto, she'd become friends with the flamboyant and rich tobacco heir Arthur Jeffress when he'd visited Redfern looking for new paintings. She was in Ascona planning the opening of a new gallery – the Hanover Gallery – which Jeffress had agreed to fund. She did not know it then, but the Hanover would quickly become famous because of the paintings – and behaviour – of one man: Francis Bacon.

The two women bonded instantly, and initially, over their shared experiences in the Paris of the 1930s, though neither of them could remember meeting the other despite moving in similar circles. But then their conversations became deeper, and when Erica heard about Toto's courage with the Resistance fighters in Italy, and the horrors of Ravensbruck, she immediately enveloped her in the warmth that Toto had sensed under the terseness. As Toto told Laura Aitken: '*Erica was so kind to me when I was still at a very low ebb. It was as if my old nanny Djim had come back to look after me.*'

Within two days the pair were inseparable.

CHAPTER 28

ENTER FRANCIS BACON

'I found it unforgivable […] he was a horrible man.'
– Toto

Two weeks after meeting, Toto and Erica left Switzerland for London. The relationship was more one of a loving mother nursing her child back to full health, which Toto, whether consciously or not, had desperately needed. Though not yet lovers, Erica was very much in love with her 'child' and it would stay that way for the rest of the lives. For Toto it was great affection, but not true love.

Erica suggested that Toto help her establish the Hanover Gallery and that they live together in her apartment in Chelsea, though much of its famous elegance had been destroyed by the Luftwaffe. At first Toto lay low, however, continuing her regime of sleeping and eating and exercising. But eventually she felt able to meet up with old friends, the first being Stewart Menzies, head of MI6, who took her to the first of many lunches as a thank you for her work with the Italian Resistance. Randolph Churchill then asked her to accompany him to the newly reopened Royal Opera House in Covent Garden, which was very much to her taste. He was still married, unhappily, but this was not a romantic outing. Randolph was genuinely concerned about his former lover. As she told Laura Aitken: *'Randolph was wonderful, always a gentleman with me, and in many ways he was my saviour. We stayed really good friends until he died in 1988.'* Sadly, he died young, aged just 57; no doubt the daily intake of two bottles of whisky and 100 cigarettes had played their part in that.

Slowly the old Toto was emerging. Her weight was almost back to normal, and her hair had grown again and was shining and lustrous. When Elizabeth Eichmann had visited she was overjoyed and said, 'She left Ravensbruck without the slightest feeling of hatred. I believe that attitude allowed her to regain a more or less normal life.' Ody stayed for four days, too, and was relieved to see how she had improved since he'd last seen her in Ascona – although he was unsure about the way Erica appeared to control everything his sister did. He had to concede, though, when he saw that her loving care was yielding great results.

Together Toto and Erica began planning the Hanover Gallery. Arthur Jeffress would join them occasionally, but he was very much a sleeping partner, providing the funds and names of potential customers. By any standards, Jeffress was different. He was born just outside London and sent to Winston Churchill's old school, Harrow. After Cambridge he inherited £8 million (in today's value) and bought an apartment in Belgravia, moving later to Portman Square – at the same time Toto had lived there with Max Aitken. He was truly one of the 'bright young things', spending much of his time in Venice. He lived the life of a prince there, employing two full-time gondoliers to ferry him and his friends to the Lido beach, where these handsome boatmen in immaculate yellow and white uniforms, monogrammed with the Jeffress crest, would serve lunch.

Erica had found suitable premises in George Street, off Hanover Square, and was in charge of putting together the exhibitions. Toto took the role of identifying invitees to the gallery's private viewings simply because, after her 12 years at the heart of society in Paris and London, she knew almost everybody: politicians, royalty, artists and aristocrats…an intoxicating mix of the powerful, the rich and the beautiful.

The Hanover opened in June 1947, and their intricate planning paid dividends. Toto had invited – penning each immaculately handwritten invitation herself – some of the best known names of the day, including Beaverbrook, who sent his apologies, and Max Aitken, who arrived with Randolph Churchill. Stewart Menzies was there, as was the ever-supportive Ody, and Elizabeth Eichmann and Cecil Beaton…the real Who's Who of British and European Establishment. Mademoiselle Chanel was not invited.

On display was the work of Graham Sutherland, then regarded as Britain's greatest artist and chosen in 1954 by the Houses of Parliament to paint an official portrait of Winston Churchill. The old man hated it, saying it made him 'look like a drunk picked out of the gutter', and later, after its display in parliament, he showed his displeasure by throwing it on a bonfire at Chartwell, his country home in Kent. The Bonfire of the Vanities… Fortunately, Sutherland's works were rather more appreciated by the guests at the Hanover's opening night.

The evening was a great success and led to a suggestion by Sutherland that Erica should put on a show by Francis Bacon. Erica knew Bacon and was keen to do just that, but not yet. There were two reasons why. Wisely, she wanted the Hanover to be firmly established before risking a Bacon exhibition, because she knew his paintings would shock. The other reason was more practical: he was yet to create enough work to show.

It was two years later, and after many a 'safe' exhibition of old masters and British artists – there were still post-war restrictions on importing art – Erica took a deep breath, and Bacon's first one-man show was launched at the Hanover in November 1949.

Toto hated Bacon immediately, both the man and his art. His paintings were unrelentingly bleak and, after the horrors she had experienced, portrayals of violence, cruelty and butchery was the last thing she needed. The feeling was mutual, but for entirely different reasons. Insanely jealous, Bacon loathed Toto because, by now, she and Erica were lovers, and called her 'the Javanese whore'. Nevertheless, Toto supported Erica in whatever she did, and tried not to show her distaste for her partner's discovery of Bacon.

Bacon was a mess. Born in Dublin, he was horsewhipped by grooms on the orders of his father, a racehorse trainer, because of his son's effeminacy. As a boy he frequently dressed up in his mother's clothes, and as a young man he lived off his mother's allowance in Berlin and Paris where, unbeknown to Toto, he had gate-crashed one of her birthday parties. He was a petty thief and rent boy, running the most appalling risks for his safety, his health and his freedom – homosexuality being a criminal offence in the UK until 1967. He was a hard and unashamed gambler, and lost huge sums in casinos, which he could not afford to repay. He was also deeply unpleasant when drunk, which he frequently was. That said, he was also well read, a *bon vivant,* and could be good company if sober. He had been 'rescued' by Erica in 1946, when she paid today's equivalent of £12,000 for *Painting*, a work the artist described as 'created by accident'. He used the money to pay off debts and to move to Monte Carlo where, inevitably, he gambled again and lost. Erica, who had seen a future for Bacon where others didn't, more than made her money back by selling *Painting* to the Museum of Modern Art in New York for an undisclosed sum.

The debut exhibition at the Hanover was crucial in establishing Bacon as one of the country's leading, albeit controversial, artists, but it didn't stop his reckless behaviour, and Erica was constantly bailing him out.

On several occasions Toto, despite her view of Bacon, journeyed to Europe to deliver cash to him, running the risk of arrest if found guilty of breaching strict currency regulations.

Nine years after his one-man show at the Hanover, Bacon repaid Erica's long-extended hand of support and kindness by leaving the gallery for the rival Marlborough Fine Art Gallery. It was an utter betrayal, and typical of the man who did not even have the courage to tell Erica to her face. The news arrived in a letter postmarked Paris.

Later Toto told Laura Aitken: '*Francis Bacon was a very troubled man, but that did not excuse his behaviour or what he did to Erica. She tried not to appear upset but she was, I knew that better than anyone. Even then, they remained on reasonable terms, though I found it unforgivable. I didn't like his paintings either, but given the price of his work now, I suppose I was in a minority. But he was a horrible man.*'

CHAPTER 29

FROM RICHES TO RICHES

'Coco Chanel is a wretched human being…'
– The New York Times

Little is known about the move, or why, but in 1948 Hans Gunther von Dincklage upped and decamped to Majorca. It would appear to have been a mutual decision, however, because Chanel paid all his expenses…for the rest of his life. Nobody seems to know if they ever met again. Was it a way of buying his continued silence, like she had Schellenberg's?

In 1953 she wrote to her friend and admirer Carmel Snow of Harper's Bazaar: 'I thought it would be fun to work again…you know, I might one day create a new style adapted to today's living.' It took some time, but on 5th February 1954 the first Chanel collection since the war opened in Paris; but it was to poor reviews from both the French and British press. America was full of praise, however, which proved to be her salvation. It seemed the fashionable east and west-coast women were the ones with the money. But it had cost her couture company £500,000, which had left these particular coffers empty.

Then Pierre Wertheimer, the man she had spent half her life fighting, stepped in again with the final deal. Two months later Chanel sold all her properties and commercial holdings to the Wertheimers; her houses in Switzerland, Paris and the South of France, her car, the fashion business and everything bearing the Chanel name. In return she could continue to live in the homes and never had to pay another bill for 17 years, in other words the rest of her life. The Wertheimers would look after all those costs which included upkeep on the properties, her Ritz suite, all travel, salaries for servants, right down to telephone and postage. Absolutely everything. She would also get a royalty on sales of her couture and perfume businesses. She would never look back...and neither would the Wertheimers.

Growing richer by the minute, Chanel went on to live a relatively uneventful life, notable only for lesbian affairs with some of her very young models, and for taking her young butler, Francois Mironnet, as her live-in lover – possibly because he bore an uncanny resemblance to Bendor Grosvenor, whom she had never really been able to forget. She would keep designing collections and developing new perfumes until the age of 71.

She was 87 when a chambermaid found her dead in bed at her Ritz suite. She had died of a heart attack in her sleep. She was alone, not surrounded by a loving family – because she didn't have a loving family.

Most of the worldwide obituaries and tributes were rightly full of admiration for one of the world's leading designers, heaping praise on her brilliance and originality: her single-mindedness had changed the way women looked, and smelled. That snap decision in 1922, when she had been faced with an array of scents and changed her mind from No 22 to No 5 had made history. Today, a bottle of Chanel No 5 sells every 55 seconds somewhere around the globe. And in the century since the perfume was launched, sales have been worth more than £24 billion in today's money. It would appear the swathes of American women who bought her designs and smothered themselves in her perfume were also unaware of her past.

In 1971, the secret papers on her wartime collaboration had not been released. And those who knew the truth had either been bought off or were dead.

The New York Times was the only paper utterly uncompromising in its opinion of Mademoiselle Chanel: '*Coco Chanel was a wretched human being. Anti-Semitic, homophobic, social climbing, opportunistic and ridiculously snobbish.*'

CHAPTER 30

TOTO, ONCE MORE AMUSED AND AMUSING

'I suppose it was my way of finally banishing the memories of Ravensbruck.'

– Toto

When Francis Bacon repaid Erica's faith, support and investment with his treachery, it was Toto's time to become the mother figure, comforting a broken Brausen with tenderness and love. Erica was on the brink of giving up the Hanover Gallery, but Toto persuaded her to keep going. They spent Christmas together in Paris, and by early January Toto felt Erica was ready to throw herself back into work.

Erica left for London, and Toto flew to Italy, where she went by ancient boat from Naples to the smallest of the remote Aeolian islands, Panarea. The voyage took an uncomfortable 18 hours, but the purpose was to see a property that was for sale, a rundown house without water, electricity or drainage on an island with no roads or beaches. Toto loved it and bought it straight away;

and just as the Hanover was Erica's project, Panarea became hers. She oversaw the entire project, and worked tirelessly with the architect to remodel the tiny island with a sensitive touch, planting jasmine, bougainvillea and tobacco flowers. She also built six cottages, and in time transformed the entire inactive volcanic island into a paradise of the most beautiful creation.

As she told Laura Aitken, '*I suppose it was my way of finally banishing the memories of Ravensbruck. Replacing something so monstrous, so ugly with a little piece of beauty.*'

Beaverbrook became a regular visitor, buying works for the Beaverbrook Art Gallery he opened in 1959 at New Brunswick, Canada. She regularly saw Max, too, her one great love, as well as a trio of eccentric gay men who would stay close to her for the rest of her life. Their company reminded her of some of the outrageous characters who'd frequented her set in pre-war Paris, except that, in contrast to the Mdivanis, these were the real deal.

The first of these was Robert Heber-Percy, a relative of the Duke of Northumberland. He had been an army officer, and was married with a daughter, but was known as Mad Boy. Together with wife and child, he lived as companion and lover with the composer Lord Berners in a grand house in Oxfordshire where guests were unsurprised, given their host's tastes, to find pink flamingos and pigeons dyed the colours of the rainbow on the lawns. Mad Boy would ride his horse through the drawing room of the house, while stark naked. Oh, and he was also an undertaker…

The second was Neil Munro Roger, known as Bunny – what else! – his face white with too much powder and whose party trick was to appear with his brothers in fancy dress as the Bronte Sisters.

But her greatest friend of these three was Kensington Davison, later the third Lord Broughshane – Ken, as he was known. Ken had been a brave and decorated war pilot and, because he spoke fluent German, later interrogated his opposite numbers from the Luftwaffe. He was also a barrister and a passionate opera lover, becoming a director of the Friends of Covent Garden. He and Toto were inseparable and an almost permanent fixture at the Royal Opera House when Toto was in London. Ken was the only person who had the dubious honour of having 'worn' a Francis Bacon painting. This came about at a Bacon collection at the Hanover, when he unknowingly leaned against an exhibit which had been finished in such a hurry that the oils were still wet. Erica footed the bill for the dry cleaning; Toto found it highly amusing.

Toto was very much back 'in character' with these three, because she had a need to be entertained by people, and to entertain.

There was one event, however, which almost unravelled her once again. Her beloved brother Ody died of a heart attack in Holland in 1949. He was her only sibling, and the sole link to her childhood in Java, memories of which seemed to both comfort and distress her in equal measure as the circumstances of her life had changed her. He'd seemed so fit last time she'd seen him, and was still playing tennis almost daily. She'd thought they would grow old together.

She decided that, to overcome her grief, she had to be even more occupied, so she enrolled at the Institute of Archaeology at London University. Her teacher was Sir Max Mallowen, husband of Agatha Christie. It is doubtful even she could have dreamed up a heroine quite like Toto.

CHAPTER 31

WHEN HER MIGHTY MEN FELL

'I have never regretted anything…'

– Toto

Toto was back with Max Aitken, no longer an MP, but a frequent visitor and client of the Hanover, where he bought works for his homes in London, the Isle of Wight, in Austria and for Cherkley. He was still working for Express Newspapers, but still had no heart for the job. His greatest passion was now powerboat racing, and sailing, and he founded the London International Boat Show in 1954 with sponsorship from Express Newspapers. Six years later he started the Cowes to Torquay powerboat race, which is still running today, and an exciting spectacle with boats hitting almost 100 miles per hour.

As for the Express titles, all was well with sales of the Daily – more than four million – but the first hint that things might be shifting came in 1957 when Arthur Christiansen, its greatest editor, had a heart attack while staying at Beaverbrook's house in the South of France. He had been at the helm for a record-breaking 24 years, but despite recovering his health Beaverbrook replaced him – to the astonishment and anger of the newspaper community.

The Beaver himself was no longer the force he had been. His political career was far behind him. His last cabinet position had been as Lord Privy Seal, but he'd lost the job when his greatest friend Churchill was defeated in the 1946 general election. On hearing the result, Beaverbrook put on a black arm band and sang the hymn 'Oh God, Our Help in Ages Past'. He didn't muster the enthusiasm or the energy to visit the Express offices again, and by 1964 he was an old and exhausted man of 85, jealously guarded over by his second wife Christofor, widow of his old friend Sir James Dunn.

Lord Thomson, his fellow Canadian-born press baron, organised a birthday party for his old friend – his 85th – at the Dorchester and, in his speech, Beaverbrook told the guests: 'First I was an apprentice in politics, next an apprentice in Fleet Street and slave to the dark arts, then came the Second World War. That was when I was an apprentice in industrial production under the guidance of Winston Churchill. Our peril was beyond comprehension and we were woefully unprepared for it. Now is the time for me to become an apprentice once again.'

This complicated, difficult, but very great man died shortly afterwards in June that year. Britain had lost a man who was outstanding by any standards. He had helped turn the tide of the World War II and was Churchill's ever-faithful sounding board. He was the driving force of his newspapers, underlined by the performance of the Express stable after his death. Circulation gradually fell throughout the 1970s and '80s under the chairmanship of a distracted Max, who had a habit of enrolling poor managers. They failed to diversify, as other newspaper groups did to great effect, notably Thomson and Associated, owners of The Times and The Sunday Times, and The Daily Mail respectively. The decline was rapid.

About the death of William Maxwell Aitken, 1st Baron Beaverbrook, Toto told Laura Aitken:

> *'Despite that row I had with him, I had such great affection for Max. He educated me in so many ways, and without him I would never have developed my interest in politics and the terrible events of the Thirties. He could be difficult, but maybe because I was young, naive even, I let it all go over my head. I probably would not have ended up in Ravensbruck if I had not been with him and been introduced to the Secret Service. But who knows? I have never regretted anything, not even that. Your grandfather was a really great man and I was privileged to have known him.'*

His son Max died in 1985 at the age of 75 after a series of strokes. Toto had lost another of the great men in her life, but Max was the only man she adored. As she'd told Laura, *'I loved Max like no other before or after and I would have married him…'*

Toto's archaeological digs in the Middle East, Greece and Turkey, and visits to her tiny idyll of Panarea had begun to upset Erica. So too had her affairs with a variety of men, among them her great friend from Italy, the journalist William Rospigliosi and, before his death, her renewed relationship with Max.

The affairs continued for years, the most surprising of which was with a handsome young member of Italy's Carabinieri force. They travelled together extensively, and for a while she even moved him into the apartment she shared with Erica – Eaton Place, Belgravia – and Erica became increasingly insecure and possessive.

Laura Aiken rang to arrange to visit Toto in 1986. She said: 'I had been going over my father's papers after he died the year before and I was intrigued to know more about this woman whom he had obviously loved. When I rang the flat she shared with Erica Brausen it was Erica who answered, and she made it clear she didn't want me to visit. Fortunately, Toto agreed.'

The reality was that, despite the affairs, Toto was never going to leave Erica, and never did. She had huge affection for her, even if it was not the intense love that Erica had for her.

Erica, however, had an assortment of medical problems by this time, and her mental health was unravelling. She was also injecting morphine, just as Coco Chanel had done for much of her life, and for the second time Toto became the mother, doing her best to care for her friend.

But then there was another sudden, tragic reversal of roles.

CHAPTER 32

NO FOND FAREWELLS

'I believe that Erica thought she finally had her to herself and would no longer share her with anyone.'
– Elizabeth Eichmann

In May 1991 Toto suffered a stroke, and she fell and broke her hip. She was taken to the Devonshire Hospital, but released after only a week. It was the worst thing that could have happened. Erica was by then quite mentally ill, and still bitterly jealous of Toto's friends, male and female, all of whom were desperate to visit. They were all refused, even Elizabeth Eichmann, who rang Erica only to be told, coldly, to stay away. Elizabeth said: 'I was not allowed to visit or even talk to her on the telephone. Her behaviour was unforgivable; it was monstrous of her to cut off Toto from her friends. I believe that Erica thought she finally had her to herself and would no longer share her with anyone.'

The once warm and caring Erica then placed Toto under the 'care' of Victor Ratner, a notorious charlatan of a physician who had been charged in 1965 under the Dangerous Drugs Act, though the case never was brought to trial. Two years later, Ratner was attacked by a coroner at the inquest of one of his patients, and he fled to Israel until the furore died down. But by 1991 he was back again, practicing as a so-called 'society doctor' – one of his patients was Elizabeth Taylor – from his rooms in Upper Wimpole Street. Ken Davison immediately stepped in and hired the trusted nurse who had looked after Toto at the Devonshire. The nurse, a Russian called Lydia, moved into Eaton Place…and was horrified to see the state Toto was in and how she was being treated by Erica and the bogus Ratner. When she had been discharged from hospital, physical exercise had been prescribed, along with the company of friends. Toto was instead confined to a dark, hot, airless room – it was the middle of August – and Ratner was injecting Toto with drugs which sent her into a stupor. Lydia's protests were met with the inevitable: Erica Brausen got rid of her.

Ken and other friends did everything they could to rescue Toto from the combined forces of Brausen and Ratner, but it was too late. At midnight on 27th August 1991 this most beautiful, brave and resourceful of women died, full of the morphine ordered by the malevolent Ratner and administered by his unwitting accomplice Erica. She was 82, and may well have had several more years left to entertain and amuse, and to be amused and entertained. But she had been killed by cruelty, neglect, and in defiance of the instructions for the fresh air, exercise and company that may well have extended her life. Toto knew only too well how these things can restore a soul.

Shockingly, Toto lay dead in her bed for eight days. Every day, Erica laid a fresh red rose on her body, and every night this increasingly insane woman slept with the corpse of the friend and lover she had helped restore, but had finally imprisoned out of jealousy. It was Ratner who signed the death certificate.

Toto Koopman was buried at East Finchley Cemetery in north London. Each of the few mourners permitted by Erica Brausen to attend was clutching a red rose.

Brausen then went back to Eaton Place and for 16 months lived as a total recluse, visited only by Ratner – who charged her £750,000 for the 'treatment' he'd administered to the beautiful woman she claimed she loved. Three years later, appropriately and maybe inevitably, Ratner died of a self-administered overdose of heroin.

EPILOGUE

Toto Koopman: adventurer, linguist, stunning beauty, the world's first bi-racial model, faithful friend, lover, socialite, art gallery pioneer, archaeologist, creator of a beautiful island…and Holocaust survivor.

All who came into contact with her were touched by her; many, men and women, fell in love with her. She was living, breathing, vibrant proof that the human spirit can overcome the darkest of hardships. Yet she was gone. Confined to a lightless room, captive once more beyond her control, when she should have been able to see and feel the green grass, sit with friends, and have the sun on her face.

It was a pitiful and needless end to the life, or rather the many lives, of the 20th century's greatest unknown freedom fighter, British spy and heroine. Her childhood celluloid heroine Pauline simply could not have matched *The Trials of Toto*.

INDEX

Several people appear throughout this book; Toto Koopman and Coco Chanel of course, but also Lord Beaverbrook, Max Aitken, Winston Churchill and Adolf Hitler. For this reason, references to them in this Index are for specific events only. You may be assured they will be present, for good or ill, constantly.

Aitken, Janet (Janet Kidd)..Chpt. 3, 5, 6, 8, 9
Aitken, Laura ....All chapters
Aitken, Sir Max
    Childhood..Chpt. 8
    Learns to fly...Chpt. 8
    Meets Toto..Chpt. 7
    Letters...Chpt. 8
    Wartime service...Chpt. 10, 14
    Later life..Chpt. 24, 25, 28, 30, 31
Aitken, William Maxwell, Lord Beaverbrook
    Childhood..Chpt. 5
    Arrives in London...Chpt. 5
    Cherkley, Stornoway House...Chpt. 5
    Epithets of friends and enemies....................................Chpt. 5, 6
    Meets Toto..Chpt. 5
    His mistresses...Chpt. 6
    Express Newspapers empire...Chpt. 3, 6, 8, 10, 31
    William Hickey Column...Chpt. 5, 6
    Letters to Max..Chpt. 8, 14
    As Cabinet Minister in both world wars.............................Chpt. 5, 14

— INDEX —

Friendship with Churchill..Chpt. 5, 10, 14

Impact on aircraft production..............................Chpt. 14

Farewell dinner speech..Chpt. 31

Peter Aitken..Chpt. 5

Aster van Alen, Louise...Chpt. 2

Asquith, HH..Chpt. 5

Bacon, Francis..Chpt. 28, 30

Bankhead, Tallulah

Childhood..Chpt, 4

Meets Toto...Chpt. 4

Eton College affair...Chpt. 4

Temple, Robert, opinion of..............................Chpt. 4

Haslam, Nicky, opinion of...............................Chpt. 4

Bate, Vera...Chpt. 3, 19, 23

Beaton, Cecil..Chpt. 2, 3, 28

Bevan, Aneurin...Chpt. 5

Bonar Law, Andrew..Chpt. 5

Bartali, Gino...Chpt. 10

Bedaux, Charles..Chpt. 9, 12

Bernodotte, Count Folke...Chpt. 22, 23

Binz, Dorothea...Chpt. 16

Bommejin de Rochement, Jeanne................................Chpt. 22

Bracken, Brendan...Chpt. 6

Brausen, Erica..Chpt. 27, 28, 30, 31, 32

Bruce Lockhart, Robert..Chpt. 9

Buber-Neumann, Margarete..Chpt. 16

Budberg, Baroness Moura...Chpt. 8, 9

Canaris, Admiral Wilhelm...Chpt. 3, 9

Campbell, Ian (Duke of Argyll)....................................Chpt. 8

Campbell, Lady Jeanne..Chpt. 6

Castlerosse, Lord (Valentine).......................................Chpt. 4, 5, 6, 7

Chanel, Gabrielle 'Coco'

Childhood..Chpt. 3

Her anti-Semitism..Chpt. 3

Beginnings of business empire..........................Chpt. 3

Capel, Arthur 'Boy'..Chpt. 3

Little Black Dress...Chpt. 3

Chanel No 5...Chpt. 3

Friendship with Churchill..................................Chpt. 3, 13, 23

Palasse, Andre (Chanel's nephew).....................Chpt. 3, 13

Pavlovich, Grand Duke Dmitri..........................Chpt. 3

Beaux, Ernest...Chpt. 3

Wertheimer, Pierre..Chpt. 3, 13, 17, 26
Affair with Duke of Westminster...........................Chpt. 3
With Dincklage...Chpt. 3, 8, 10, 12, 13, 19,
                                                                                23, 26, 28
Operation Modelhut..Chpt. 19
In Paris after Liberation.......................................Chpt. 21
Flees to Switzerland..Chpt. 23
Final years...Chpt. 26, 29
Chamberlain, Neville...Chpt. 9, 10, 14
Christiansen, Arthur..Chpt. 5, 31
Churchill, Clementine..Chpt. 3, 19
Churchill, Randolph...Chpt. 3, 6, 7, 8, 24, 25, 28
Churchill, Winston...Chpt. 3, 6, 8, 13, 14, 19, 23
Ciano, Count Gian...Chpt. 10
Clauberg, Carl..Chpt. 20
Colville, Jock (Churchill's private secretary)...................Chpt. 7, 14
Curteis, Lady Deirdre..Chpt. 3, 4, 12
Davison, Kensington (Lord Broughshane).....................Chpt. 30
Delevingne, Doris (Lady Castlerosse)............................Chpt. 6, 7
Della Costa, Elia (Archbishop of Florence)....................Chpt. 10, 11
Delmer, Sefton..Chpt. 5, 9
Dincklage, Baron Hans Gunther von (known as Spatz)...Chpt. 3, 8, 12, 13, 19, 23,
                                                                                26, 28
Dincklage, Maximiliane (known as Catsy).....................Chpt. 3
De Vaufreland, Baron Louis..Chpt. 13, 17, 21, 23
Driberg, Tom..Chpt. 6
Eichmann, Elizabeth...Chpt. 11, 5, 16, 24, 28
Foot, Michael...Chpt. 6
Gebhardt, Karl...Chpt. 20
Giles, Carl..Chpt. 6
Goebbels, Joseph..Chpt. 3, 9, 12, 15
Goering, Hermann...Chpt. 8
Goldwyn, Samuel...Chpt. 3
Grandi, Count Dino..Chpt. 10
Halifax, Lord..Chpt. 14
Hearst, Bill...Chpt. 8
Hearst, Randolph..Chpt. 8
Heber-Percy, Robert (Mad Boy)...................................Chpt. 30
Himmler, Heinrich..Chpt. 16, 18, 19, 20, 22
Hitler, Adolf...Chpt. 8, 19, 12, 22
Hoare, Sir Samuel...Chpt. 19
Honnegar, Franz...Chpt. 9

— INDEX —

Hoskins, Percy..Chpt. 5

Hoyningen-Huene, George...Chpt. 2

Hutton, Barbara...Chpt. 2

Iribe, Paul...Chpt. 11

Jeffress, Arthur...Chpt. 28

Junor, John...Chpt. 5, 8

Keeble, Harold..Chpt. 5

Kenworthy, Jonathan...Chpt. 5

Kipling, Rudyard...Chpt. 5

Koopman

    Jan George (father)..Chpt. 1

    Catharina (mother)..Chpt. 1

    Ody (brother)....................................Chpt. 1, 24, 27, 28

Koopman, Toto

    Meets Max...Chpt. 7

    Her trips to Germany and Italy.............Chpt. 8, 9, 10, 11, 12

    Joins Italian Resistance..Chpt. 11

    Imprisoned in Italy...Chpt. 12, 14

    Dinner with gauleiter..Chpt. 15

    Taken to Ravensbruck..Chpt. 16

    In Ravensbruck...Chpt. 16 – 22

    Freedom...Chpt. 22

    In Switzerland...Chpt. 24, 25

    Meets Erica Brausen...Chpt. 27

    Returns to London..Chpt. 27

    With Hanover Gallery.....................................Chpt. 27, 28

    Dislike of Francis Bacon......................................Chpt. 28

    In Panarea..Chpt. 30

    Final years..Chpt. 31, 32

    Imprisoned again..Chpt. 32

Mainbocher...Chpt. 2

Maisky, Ivan (Soviet ambassador to London)..................Chpt. 5

Mallowen, Sir Max..Chpt. 30

Menkel, Albert..Chpt. 15

Menzies, Sir Stuart...Chpt. 5, 9

Mountbatten, Lord...Chpt. 5

Mountbatten, Lady...Chpt. 5

Mozzi, Leonardo...Chpt. 11

Mussolini. Benito.....................................Chpt. 10, 12, 15

Norton, Jean (Lady Grantley).......................................Chpt. 5

Oberheuser, Dr Herta..Chpt. 20

Picchi, Fortunato..Chpt. 11

Pincher, Harry Chapman..Chpt. 5

Rado, Lorenzo..Chpt. 11

Raffles, Sir Stamford..Chpt. 1

Ratner, Victor...Chpt. 32

Ravensbruck concentration camp................................Chpt. 16 – 22

Ribbentrop, Joachim von...Chpt. 8, 19

Rochas..Chpt. 2

Rospiglioni, William..Chpt. 12, 24

Rothermere, Lord..Chpt. 8

Schellenberg, Walter (SS general)................................Chpt. 19, 22, 26

Sert, Josep Maria..Chpt. 8, 21

Simon, Sir John..Chpt. 3

Suhren, Fritz..Chpt. 17

Thomas, Gregory..Chpt. 17

Thyssen, Maud...Chpt. 2

Tribich, Mala...Chpt. 16

Vansittart, Sir Robert...Chpt. 5

Wallace, Brian..Chpt. 13

Wardell, Mike...Chpt. 8

Wells, HG..Chpt. 5

Wenner-Gren, Axel..Chpt. 9

Westminster, Duke of...Chpt. 3, 11, 19, 23

Windsor, Duke of (Prince of Wales)..............................Chpt. 3, 9, 12, 14, 23

BIBLIOGRAPHY

Jean-Noel Liaut, *The Many Lives of Miss K* (Rizzoli), 2011

Hal Vaughan, *Sleeping with the Enemy* (Vintage), 2012

Sarah Helm, *If This is a Woman* (Hachette), 2016

Caroline Moorehead, *A House in the Mountains* (Vintage), 2019

Anne Chisholm and Michael Davie, *Beaverbrook, A Life* (Random House), 1992

Charles Williams, *Max Beaverbrook, Not Quite a Gentleman* (Biteback), 2019

Andrew Lownie, *The Mountbattens, Their Lives and Loves* (Blink), 2019

Peter Hore, *Lindell's List* (The History Press), 2016

Logan Gourlay, *The Beaverbrook I Knew* (Quartet), 1984

Janet Kidd, *The Beaverbrook Girl* (Collins), 1987

Erik Larson, *The Splendid and the Vile* (William Collins), 2020

Roderick Bailey, *Target Italy* (Faber and Faber) 2014

Joel Lobenthal, *Tallulah!* (Harper Collins), 2008

Tallulah Bankhead, *My Autobiography* (University Press of Mississippi), 1952

Richard Bassett, *Hitler's Spy Chief* (Weidenfeld and Nicholson), 2005

Lord Beaverbrook's Personal Papers, House of Lords' Archive, various years

THE AUTHOR

Alan Frame is a journalist, broadcaster and author. He has worked for the London Evening News, Daily Mail and Daily Express where, until 1995, he was executive editor. He also had a weekly news review show on LBC. From 1995-98 he was CEO of Liberty Publishing, a division of Harrods Holdings.

Printed in Great Britain
by Amazon